TRUEMAN'S TALES

John Morgan and David Joy

GREAT NORTHERN

Publisher's note

This book began as a series of lengthy and memorable interviews that David Joy had with Fred Trueman in the first half of 2006. They were intended to form the basis of a collection of his humorous tales of life on and off the pitch. Then came Fred's untimely death, and it soon became apparent that many of his sporting colleagues and close friends wished to contribute to a work now clearly destined to form a tribute to a remarkable man.

John Morgan, the sports journalist who knew Fred over many years, has accordingly written a greatly enlarged text. The tributes in the first section, 'The Man with a Million Fans', are expressed in their own words by those who contributed them, but otherwise all first-person references are to John.

Trueman's Tales, the title originally envisaged for the book and the one agreed with Fred, has been retained. The anecdotes are not only those told by Fred, but also embrace the many more tales and memories told about a much-loved Yorkshireman.

Great Northern Books
PO Box 213, Ilkley, LS29 9WS
www.greatnorthernbooks.co.uk

© John Morgan and David Joy 2007

Photographs courtesy Yorkshire Post Newspapers and Veronica Trueman.

Every effort has been made to acknowledge correctly and contact the copyright holders of material in this book. Great Northern Books Ltd apologises for any unintentional errors or omissions, which should be notified to the publisher.

ISBN: 978 1 905080 22 9

Design and layout: David Burrill

Printed in Spain

CIP Data
A catalogue for this book is available from the British Library

CONTENTS

Fred Trueman, painted by John Blakey in 1986.

Prologue

'Yorkshire and Cricket Has Been My Life'

No player since the war, especially as a bowler, has captured the popular imagination as much as Trueman. He is known as one of the best triers the game has ever produced. His figures speak for themselves.

Trueman always makes his presence felt but, in the way that all the world loves a rebel, so the crowds love Trueman the man. He is seldom relaxed. His dark flashing eyes continually on the move. Energetic, voluble and volatile, the smallest thing finds full support or complete disappointment, and the man at the receiving end, whether he be an opposing batsman or a colleague, is likely to remember it. The powerful, full-bodied menace in his bowling attack has won him universal admiration. The strength of his verbal attack has made him enemies.

If there is anybody to listen he hardly stops talking for a moment. On his walk back to the bowling mark he sometimes stops to tell the non-striker: "I'll pin that pal of yours to the sightscreen" and the direction of his thumb dictates he means the batsman at the striker's end.

He cocks a snook at authority. He can be led but unwillingly driven. His cricket philosophy is easily understood by adult and schoolboy alike because every ball is an instrument of destruction. He wields a bat like a club and is prepared to hit or be hit. Fred's father, Alan Thomas Trueman, was a well-known, local, left-arm bowler and batsman and, said Fred with real sincerity: "I owe everything to him. He was the one who encouraged me when nothing seemed to go right. He never lost faith in me and, but for him, I would have been a miner working with him down the pit."

When Fred said this he looked at me and grinned: "Aye, and probably you never lost faith in me, Bill."

It was as near to saying something nice as Fred could ever get and, almost to hide it, he hurried on.

"But I don't regret one minute of my time at cricket. The game's been good to me. I've travelled and met some grand folk. When I came off the ground after bowling Australia out at Headingley, I had such a reception from t'crowd I couldn't have felt more proud if I'd been made King."

Fred was certainly the King of Headingley that day.

During his time with Yorkshire, Fred had no fewer than twenty-seven other bowlers to open the attack with him. He kept remarkably free from injury and saw them all off. His right to the new ball and the first over was never challenged.

The man who gave pleasure to thousands murmured: "If I had my time to come over again I would do the same thing. Yorkshire and cricket has been my life."

Bill Bowes – Fred Trueman's mentor – writing in 1962

Fred Trueman and his mentor Bill Bowes had more in common than sincere love of the game, both adorned as England and Yorkshire fast bowlers. Fred delighted in releasing rocket-like deliveries at international level and, likewise, Bill shared the pace attack with legendary Harold Larwood and Bill Voce on the infamous bodyline tour to Australia.

Another common denominator was an addiction to the briar. Fred and Bill could have smoked for Britain. In partnership, they produced smoke screens designed to rival London 'pea-soupers'. In 1973 Fred was elected 'Pipeman of the Year' and he was installed in office by outgoing top-smoker Frank Muir of TV script fame. Runners-up for the title were eccentric astronomer Patrick Moore and sweater-clad crooner Val Doonican.

At that time Fred had a collection of over sixty pipes and he once told me that he also had a weakness for watches with dozens of them showing different times and ticking away in a rarely opened drawer.

'The Old Bill' was Fred's nickname for Bowes, the man who helped him to improve his rhythmic and explosive action designed to shatter the confidence and stumps of opposing batsmen.

Bill became an authoritative journalist when he retired from bowling and coaching. Years later Fred followed his tutor into the newspaper world with articles in the Sunday People. They were eagerly awaited by readers, who welcomed his predilection for telling the unvarnished facts. He called a spade a shovel. He was controversial and he expounded opinion not always popular with the game's hierarchy.

Bill was also widely read in the Yorkshire Evening News and later the Yorkshire Evening Post. The story was told that he charged "a bob a word" when he first contributed stories to newspapers and when one wag gave him a shilling and asked for "a unit of speech". Bill answered: "Thanks."

Locked in the 'Bowes Museum' of newspaper cuttings is a feature produced in June 1962 when Fred was rewarded for "eleven years of outstanding service" with a benefit season and a match between Yorkshire and regular rivals Surrey.

Bill and I shared a desk at the Yorkshire Evening Post at that time and he produced his stories on a battered Remington typewriter – at least twenty years older than Fred. The tops of keys were missing and he glued coins on to take the place of the absent letters. It was on this ancient machine he produced an appraisal of Fred and one I never tire of reading. It forms the prologue to this book.

Fred was a life member of the MCC and he was proud to be included on a unique painting of fellow members.

Back row (left to right): W J Edrich, K F Barrington, Sir Leonard Hutton and J C Laker.
Front (left to right): T G Evans, T E Bailey, P B H May, J B Statham, D C S Compton,
A V Bedser, Sir Colin Cowdrey, F S Trueman, E R Dexter, and T W Graveney.

There was a no more sincere 'mutual admiration duo' than that formed by Brian Close and Fred Trueman.

Brian said: "Fred was one of the world's greatest fast bowlers. He could swing better than Glenn Miller."

Fred said: "It was a privilege to play under Brian's captaincy. He was inspirational. He led by example and it was a tragedy when he left our county to play for Somerset."

Fred and Brian were youths when they joined the Yorkshire ranks. They grew and prospered together. Fred was an ever-present at the annual Brian Close Charity Golf Tournament, which has raised thousands of pounds for 'Heartbeat'.

Brian said: "We will miss Fred – not only for his golfing expertise but his fun and jokes at the dinner."

Part 1

The Man with a Million Fans

Memories from Fred Trueman's close colleagues – on and off the field

BRIAN CLOSE

The Priory Church of St Mary and St Cuthbert at Bolton Abbey was an appropriate place to bid farewell to Frederick Sewards Trueman where he and his widow Veronica had been regular worshippers for decades.

Brian Close was among the mourners and he echoed the view of many with the simple comment: "It is a sad day . . . a very sad day for family and friends, cricket, England and Yorkshire."

None knew Fred better than Brian who recalls that they were raw youngsters when they joined the Yorkshire Under-18 side at Headingley in 1948:

Our county coaches, Bill Bowes, Arthur Mitchell and Maurice Leyland, watched and marvelled at Freddie's beautiful action even at that early stage of his career. His cart-wheeling side-on release of the ball was so natural that he actually needed very little tuition and coaching. We made our first class debut together at Fenners and Fred's great sense of humour was soon apparent. He put down a pretty hard chance and turned to skipper Norman Yardley and asked: "What's this batsman using - a steel bat?"

It became apparent in those early days that his bowling was stupendous in its ferocity. The Indian batsmen of 1952 had no counter to his speed and lift. No one in Yorkshire could understand why he didn't play more times for England in the early part of his career. People moaned because we hadn't got anyone to 'give it back' to the Australian pacemen Lindwall and Miller. They bombarded England batsmen and when Fred emerged he was not an automatic choice to represent his country. He was left out of the MCC team to Australia in 1954-55, and to South Africa two years later.

It was inevitable that I would get to know Fred well. He developed an image which betrayed him. He was a bit rough, forthright and strong-willed as a young man. But he took the blame for a lot of things done by other folk. People were quick to say he was difficult to handle but I wouldn't say there was a frictional atmosphere when he played under me for Yorkshire. You had to sense his moods. Sometimes you needed to get at him. Then he would work himself up and play magnificently. On other days, a bit of leg-pulling did the trick.

We had several disagreements, particularly over tactics, for he was a very keen student of the game. We had rows but they were rows between two self-respecting men, with mutual respect for each other. And Fred was a great help to me. We had different views but we shared a common ambition to fight for Yorkshire. We wanted to keep Yorkshire cricket at the top.

Not many cricket followers realised Freddie suffered disappointment with great sensitivity. If he was going through a bad spell, or had been dropped, it meant personal failure to him and he felt things very deeply. He loved cricket company and Yorkshire profited from his wit on and off the field. If the boys were grumpy or feeling low Fred had the knack of lifting the pressure or tension.

There are many stories told about Fred, some genuine, and others completely manufactured. But Brian remembers one with immense glee:

We bumped into a cricket know-all in a hotel in Hampshire. Fred asked the rather stuffy gentleman: "If you know so much, who was the only English captain to tour Australia and New Zealand and never played in a Test match?"

There was a long silence before Fred gave the answer: "Captain Cook."

Without doubt, Fred was the greatest fast bowler I've played with. His out-swinger was the most vital part of his armament. Whatever he bowled, the delivery had perfect execution. His bouncer was vicious and forced batsmen to duck late and sometimes the wrong way. Until the front foot bowling law was introduced, his yorker destroyed the world's best batsmen.

Above all he had the classic character of the finest fast bowlers. He wanted to bowl fast. He had a great heart and could sense the moment in a big match when to unleash something really destructive.

When he began in the game he was a sloppy fielder but he finished up as a remarkable catcher close to the wicket and with a powerful throw-in with either arm, even from the outfield. He was a belligerent batsman, with many more shots than people gave him credit for.

It was a privilege to know and play with Fred and my view is that, sadly, England may never again produce another fast bowler like him.

RAYMOND ILLINGWORTH

It was former fast bowler Chris Old's benefit season and the organisers asked me to field the John Morgan All-Stars Cricket Team against the might of Yorkshire CCC, at Park Avenue, Bradford. Chris had recruited nearly a full first team of county players including Geoffrey Boycott and we realised that the odds were stacked against our comparatively inexperienced charity team. But we had one secret weapon – a former England and Yorkshire star who was working at Leicester CCC.

The match started in sunshine but rain threatened and the decision was made to reduce the overs to forty each side. Geoffrey opened the innings and he was on the thirteen mark when he mis-hit a slow delivery bowled by Rugby League player, Peter Astbury. : 'The famed England opener skied his shot and waiting to take the catch was the Roundhay, Yorkshire and England Rugby Union star, Richard Cardus. He admitted that he was trembling as he waited for the ball to arrive safely in his hands.

But Astbury had no similar feelings. He was elated and ran from the scene and leaped every step to the pavilion where he rang his wife Maureen and shouted: "I've copped Boycott." Peter was back on the field before Geoffrey had reached the boundary and the Rugby League man has dined out on the story of his unexpected triumph ever since.

Yorkshire made a decent score after Geoffrey's departure and we were left with somewhere in the region of 170 runs to win the game. Geoffrey left the ground early. He went for a net at Headingley and the following day he hit a century at Harrogate.

We were able to produce our surprise all-rounder Raymond Illingworth who had not held a bat for nearly twelve months. But he was in devastating form. He enjoyed the battle with his old club and he finished 70 not out and hammered the winning runs with a mighty six-hit.

It was such a surprise victory that the result was broadcast on Look North and Calendar the same evening. The day finished with a dinner and Fred Trueman and Mike Cowan were in fine verbal form with hilarious speeches compensating for the failure of their former Yorkshire colleagues to beat the weak opposition.

Raymond Illingworth recalled the event – and his impressive performance – when I called at his Farsley home to talk about his long and successful association with the late Fred:

My relationship with Fred started in 1949 when we were chosen to play for Yorkshire Boys on a tour to Middlesex and Sussex. Brian Close was also in the team and, believe it or not, Brian was a faster bowler than Fred in those early days. We boarded the coach and this was my first view of Fred. His first view of me resulted in him holding me out of the coach to be sick. I was always travel sick on buses.

Later I played a couple of matches in the Yorkshire second team with Fred and he did

14

Raymond Illingworth, who was described by Fred as "a world-class all-rounder and a great captain". Yorkshire lost his services when they refused him a two-year contract. Fred added: "All he wanted was security for his family. He must have been heartbroken to leave the county side he loved. Raymond didn't do badly for Leicestershire. Under his captaincy they won trophies. He also went on to skipper England and we won back the Ashes."

Previous page: Four 'Yorkshire greats' – Raymond Illingworth, Fred Trueman and Geoffrey Boycott (seated, left to right), and Brian Close (standing). Painted by John Blakey in 2005.

not always get things right at the beginning of his cricket career. I remember playing in one match at Thirsk where wicket-keeper Jackie Firth was like a goalkeeper because Fred's bowling was all over the place. Fred would never admit to that but he sent one down the legside, one down the off, and he had little idea of direction.

But he cured this fault in double quick time and within twelve months his deliveries were perfect and spot on. He had a truly wonderful action and people who did not see him play in his heyday recently had the opportunity to judge his bowling style with the television replays accompanying news of his untimely death. They will understand why we talk about side-on bowling because nobody does it these days. They should do because fast bowlers are more prone to injury and don't even bowl half as many overs as Fred did in a season.

Fred had one serious injury in 1949 when he ruptured his spleen and it was thought that his career had come to a premature end. But he had the full winter off and returned to action ready for the fray. The only other setback was a bad blister on his big toe and I don't think he missed a couple of games in twenty years. That is incredible when you consider the depth of activity with ball and bat. He bowled more than a thousand overs every season in county cricket and then went on tour. He bowled in all the fixtures abroad including the Tests. He was always given plenty to do and he appeared to thrive on hard work.

When I reflect on his early days I now realise the brilliance of his bowling and it was only in the last two years of his career that he lost a bit of pace. He still had the beautiful action and the fact that he could swing the ball at medium pace enabled him to continue taking wickets. He was still a great bowler in his advancing years.

One of his best performances was at The Oval. It was 85 degrees, hot and sticky, and he bowled off his shorter run and collected seven wickets in each innings. This was achieved with swing bowling and was something fast men like Frank Tyson could not do. If Fred had wanted to continue his career at medium pace he would have lasted at least another two years with Yorkshire. But mentally he would not have liked that because he was a fast bowler, first and foremost, and he knew when it was time to retire.

Fred was past his best when Chris Old came on the scene and we could appreciate the difference. He made Fred look medium pace but Fred still had the guile and movement of ball to take wickets.

We loved Fred because he was a born entertainer, although not in the Johnnie Wardle manner. Johnnie's fun was visual and Fred's verbal. On rainy days, when hours were spent in the dressing room, Fred and his co-opening bowler Mike Cowan would produce hours of jokes and never repeated themselves. This gift was to fashion the careers of both Fred and Mike in later days when they moved on to the after-dinner speaking circuit.

Fred was not the biggest mixer in the Yorkshire team. He wasn't one for being out with the lads or standing in a bar knocking back pints. He was a big name and if he were in his pomp today he would have been a mega, mega, star earning a million and more a year. In our days he managed to earn something in the region of nine grand a year to our one and a half. He had different connections and knew more people. He was inclined to spend a lot of time on his own but he was a person people wanted to see. He had an income from advertising and other sources but there was one thing he did lack and that was punctuality.

Fred did not know the meaning of the word and I will never forget my first Test assignment. I was told to report to Birmingham no later than 2 pm and Fred offered to pick me up at 12 noon. He said: "It won't take me two hours down the motorway."

When the clock showed 12.20 I began to worry. In fact I was panicking and rang his then wife Enid at home in York. She said: "Fred won't be long. He has just popped into the local garage for a couple of new tyres to be fitted."

We received the biggest rollicking ever from the selector Gubby Allen but I was OK because he knew I had been kept waiting for Fred who always struggled to be on time.

He was sent home for being late at one Yorkshire match by captain Vic Wilson, who was right to take this action because it wasn't the first time. Fred was constantly late and that day was the last straw for Vic. He asked what he should do and, in honesty, I told Vic that if he wanted the respect of the other players he had to take the appropriate action. One man can upset a team and Fred was late so many times. He was a senior player and set a bad example. There was a possibility that he might have lost his job but the matter was eventually sorted and Fred resumed his career.

Fred was a one-off. He was a legend and it would be impossible to count how much time he spent in the opposition dressing room. There were occasions when we sent his bag into the changing room occupied by our rivals. It was all a ruse and Fred gained wickets by his behaviour. I can still see him puffing on his pipe and saying to a young player: "I haven't heard of you. Can you hook? You'll get plenty of chance to do so out there."

This gamesmanship did not exactly do the morale or confidence of eighteen year olds much good. Fred put fear into many opposing players. He was very strong, in fact tremendously strong and, after a long spell of bowling, he would rest. Batsmen would try to take the mickey. But Fred always had something in reserve. He would still have a couple of really fast overs up his sleeve and he would let the jokers have it. Not many took a rise out of Fred, believe me. Only one or two tried and they came off second best.

I think he made his peace with Geoff Boycott. When one gets into the seventies we tend to mellow and realise how precious life is. I know he was truly sorry that Geoffrey had cancer and they did speak quite frequently.

Fred and Geoffrey were different in the way they played the game. When Fred first arrived at Headingley he didn't know which end of the bat to hold. Send him a straight ball and he was out. But, by the end of his career, he could take bowlers apart and it was difficult for him to appreciate how Geoffrey approached his own challenge.

Geoffrey was entirely different. I think he was mentally afraid of failing. He had the ability but I reasoned he was frightened to take a chance for fear of being out. He had to work hard on his game. He wasn't a natural player. He was the best manufactured batsman in the world. He didn't drink. We didn't see much of him at night. He was a loner and seemed to shut himself off from the other members of the team. It was his way of life, and lonely.

I couldn't have played for twenty years with that attitude. But we are all different. Geoffrey would shut himself off in his own private world and Fred could not appreciate or understand this lifestyle. However, Geoffrey did visit him when cancer was diagnosed and all who knew and admired Fred prayed for the recovery denied to one of the greatest fast bowlers the sport has known.

In the mid-sixties, Fred and I were left out of tours we both should have made. At the time I was definitely the best all-rounder in the country and Fred was at his fiery best. I had 1,600 runs against Fred Titmus's 1,000 and I also had 120 wickets at a cost of 17 apiece. I should have walked into the side, but Titmus made the trip.

Fred summed the situation up with a succinct view: "We don't talk with a plum in the mouth. Those who do went. We don't and we stayed at home."

We agreed on one point. We were very proud to gain our first England caps and even more elated to receive our Yorkshire caps. We loved playing for our county as well as our country.

Fred had to ask for his county cap. So did I. There was no pomp or ceremony. Fred took his home to his proud father Alan. When he died the Yorkshire cap was placed in his coffin.

I miss Fred. We all do.

GEOFF COPE

England and Yorkshire spin bowler Geoff Cope, who became chairman of the Yorkshire County Cricket Club committee when he retired from the game, is still serving Yorkshire on the admin side. He is Yorkshire's Director of Operations and he has been a true servant of the club he joined as a youth.

Geoff fulfilled three sporting ambitions and recalls them with joyful satisfaction and no small measure of nostalgia. He achieved his boyhood aim to play for Yorkshire in the same team as his hero Fred Trueman. His other idols were John Holmes, of everlasting Leeds Rugby League fame, and Eddie Gray, who displayed his soccer magic for Leeds United:

I have happy memories of the trio and enjoyed a strong friendship with each of them. We were, of course, shocked at Fred's passing. I thought he was indestructible.

Fred was definitely the best fast bowler in my youth and I will never forget his performance in one match at Eastbourne where Sussex were apparently romping to victory over Yorkshire. Sussex needed 380 to win. They were 330 for five and Parks and Griffiths had each hit a century and were going great guns. Their success seemed assured but Fred took off his sweater and said to me: "Give me the ball. I'll have a go at them."

Fred proceeded to produce the fastest four overs imaginable. He was brilliant and when he took his sweater he was almost exhausted. He was in the twilight of his career but somehow he had summoned up four overs of lightning speed. When Fred retired from the fray Sussex were nine wickets down and he tossed the ball to me and said: "Go finish them off!"

I did as I was told and Yorkshire won, thanks to Fred's Herculean effort. Where his speed and energy came from the Lord only knows. It was the performance of a truly great bowler and a magnificent competitor.

I remember another match against Essex when Keith Boyce bowled at me and made life distinctly uncomfortable. Keith hit me in several areas and appeared to have some sort of macabre satisfaction from raising bumps and bruises on my anatomy.

Fred was batting at the other end. He sympathised with my situation and advised Keith to simply bowl a straight one which would have been good enough to take my wicket. But Keith persisted to pepper me and Fred with short deliveries and we were not amused. In fact, Fred was hopping mad. He was in an even worse mood when Keith said: "They tell me you used to be a bit of a quickie Fred!"

When Keith batted the following day Fred peeled off his Yorkshire sweater and for three overs he put the Essex man to the sword. Fred was at his deadliest. He hit Keith everywhere before flattening his stumps. Keith had to pass Fred on his way back to the pavilion and I heard the Yorkshireman murmur: "Yes – I used to be a bit quick Keith!"

When Fred retired from the Yorkshire scene he played for Derbyshire in one-day games. I was in the Yorkshire dressing room when Fred walked in. He spent more time with us that he did with his Derbyshire team mates. In fact we saw more of him that day that we ever did when he turned out for Yorkshire. It was his habit to visit the opposition if only to put the fear of God into them with such promises as "You'll be doing a lot of ducking and diving today when you are not hooking the ball!"

I also remember Fred for his kindness to young players and the encouragement and advice he gave freely to lads in the early days of their respective careers. I was playing in the Yorkshire second team at Jesmond Dene when the call came for me to join the first team at Bath. Brian Close was on skipper duty with the England team and Fred was captain of Yorkshire in the absence of his great colleague.

I caught a train to Bath and when I arrived at the hotel Fred was sitting with the night porter waiting for me. He wanted to make sure that I had arrived safely and that I had a room. He also told the hotel staff to allow me to have another hour in bed the following morning because of my late arrival.

Fred was an extra special captain and his handling of young players like me, Chris Old, Peter Stringer and other colts was almost fatherly. It was a side of Fred few people saw. He constantly reminded us, and also seasoned players, that no one was bigger than the team. He also let us know how honoured we were to wear the Yorkshire blazer.

There was one hiccup in my career when I was subjected to filmed scrutiny. Our club secretary Joe Lister was rather suspicious when Fred invited me to take refuge at his

Geoff Cope, who achieved his boyhood aim to play for Yorkshire in the same team as his hero Fred Trueman. He is now Yorkshire CCC's Director of Operations.

house. At that time Fred was cricket correspondent with The People and Joe feared that he was chasing an exclusive interview with me about my problems. But Joe was wrong. There wasn't a word about me in Fred's weekly contribution to the Sunday paper.

What he did do was take me under his wing. He hid me from the media boys and told me to spend a few days with the old Yorkshire spinner, Johnnie Wardle. Fred was confident that Johnnie would solve my problem. And he did.

At that time the two other spinners, Jim Laker and Fred Titmus, also offered to iron out my action blip but Fred's advice was good enough for me. It was spot on and I benefited from a few days with Johnnie at his Thorne, Doncaster home and I was back playing for my county in double-quick time. Fred saw to that.

Fred was a great tactician who not only bowled with frightening speed but would exploit flaws in the make-up of any batsmen. We played Northants at Bramall Lane and that great batsman and character Colin Milburn was 80 not out at lunch. I put on my blazer – Yorkshire lads always did – and headed for the steak and kidney pie usually served up at this venue.

Everyone in cricket knew about my appetite and I was ravenous when I approached the dining room. But Fred pulled me back and asked: "How are you going to get Colin out?"

I was more interested in the pie and told Fred; "I'll be bowling off to middle."

Fred said: "Not this time you won't."

The steak pie was still waiting when Fred demonstrated that I would "tuck the ball under Colin".

It was the first time I had heard the expression. Then Fred explained: "Colin has a big belly. You tuck the ball under and up him. Do you see?"

It was then I did justice to the steak and kidney pie. When play was resumed Colin took guard to go for his century and Fred motioned to me to "tuck the ball under him". I did and lost sight of the ball, which finished in our wicketkeeper Jimmy Binks's safe gloves. Colin was out, caught Binks, bowled Cope.

When Colin walked by me to return to the Bramall Lane changing room he said: "Keep taking the advice from that old bugger Fred and you'll get a lot more wickets."

He knew that Fred had played a part in his dismissal.

With Fred's death not only have we lost an institution of the game – we have lost a knowledge that was so valuable to the game of cricket. On a personal front, he helped me greatly when I was a youngster and when I first came into the Yorkshire side. He will never be forgotten by me and thousands of others.

This grip launched thousands of overs and took 2,304 wickets in First Class matches. On twenty-five occasions Fred collected ten wickets in a game and he recorded four hat-tricks.

Fred Trueman never tried to hide the fact that Yorkshire county players did not always enjoy a trouble-free relationship. He admitted: "We often had a rumpus and a fall-out in the dressing room. But when we went on the field all differences, petty or otherwise, were shelved. We were united in the very bond that playing for our great county engendered. Yorkshire came first and personal problems were left in the changing room."

Fred added: "We played as a team and not individuals. It didn't matter who was making the runs or who was taking the wickets. We were a force pulling in the same direction and this made us formidable opposition for any rival counties. We had a great skipper in Brian Close, who played hell with anyone who didn't pull his weight.

Raymond Illingworth was another brilliant captain with the ability to extract the most from his players and it was a great shame that he and Brian were forced into joining other counties."

The side in this picture was a mixture of brilliant batsmen, great bowlers and terrific fielders. The maxim that 'catches win matches' was always prevalent in the Yorkshire players' midst and they had a world-class slip fielder in Phil Sharpe (left on the back row) with Don Wilson, John Waring, John Hampshire, Geoffrey Boycott and Doug Padgett. On the front row (left) are Jimmy Binks, Fred Trueman, Brian Close, Raymond Illingworth and Ken Taylor.

Fred said: "This team would give any county and even international sides a run for their money.

DICKIE BIRD

It was a privilege and an emotional experience for Dickie Bird to stand in the pulpit at the tiny church of St Mary's, Bolton Abbey, and pay tribute to his friend and cricketing colleague Fred Trueman:

The invitation to take part in the service was one I wouldn't even consider refusing, although I knew it would be impossible for me to keep back the tears.

Our friendship goes back to teenager days. We are both sons of miners and this possibly had a bearing on our relationship. We were good mates for decades even though Fred never did me any favours when I was an opposing batsman. It was everyman for himself when you faced a Trueman thunderbolt and one of them nearly put me in hospital.

Fred was doing his National Service and when he had a weekend pass he played for the Leeds team. I was an opening batsman with Barnsley and so was Michael Parkinson – the great journalist and broadcaster. Mind you, he wasn't great in those early days. He was a junior at the Barnsley Chronicle and also worked at the Doncaster office of the Yorkshire Evening Post.

We both knew of Fred's burgeoning reputation as a quickie because we had both been at Headingley nets hoping to find a place in the Yorkshire County set-up. But we were ready for him when he embarked on his first over against me. By God he was fast. He ripped one at me, which hit me just below my heart and I went down on my knees. Michael came over and hauled me to my feet. He did a silly thing like putting the bat back in my hand and I had to face Fred again.

I do remember that Michael stood at the non-striking end giggling at my unhappy experience. Fred turned to him and asked: "What are you laughing at?"

Michael replied: "Nothing Mr Trueman", and Fred said: "Don't laugh because you're next." And he was!

Dickie and Fred became close friends when the man destined to become the world's most famous umpire was chosen to play for the county both of them loved:

Fred was kind to me. He drove a car and used to give me a lift to matches and bring me home again. In those days we didn't have motorways and our journeys from games in the south always resulted in a late trip home.

I remember Fred arriving at our house at half-past two in the morning just as my dad James Harold Bird was getting up to go on the day shift at Bretton Colliery. When I introduced Fred to my dad he was over the moon. Fred was his hero and he worshipped him. He was also proud of me and perhaps my greatest regret is that he never saw me umpire. He died the year before I officiated at my first top class match in 1969.

Dickie Bird is not a gambler. He is a regular guest at York races and invariably advises the general company to place their money in the building society. He says: "It is safer than risking it with a bookmaker."

But a couple of years ago Dickie decided to take notice of the Newmarket trainer Sir Michael Stoute, who is also a cricket buff and a great admirer of the retired umpire.

"Have a good bet on my horse," advised Sir Michael, and Dickie – to his great amazement – won a tidy sum.

All in earshot quickly knew of Dickie's windfall. He stood in the winners' enclosure with Sir Michael, jockey Kieran Fallon and me. He was ashen faced and not with the amount of money he had won but the fact that he had been persuaded to produce cash from his pocket and risk having a wager.

However, I owe Dickie – not money but a thousand thanks because he saved my life. Well he says he did. I was taking steroids on my doctor's advice and so was Dickie. We both suffered from dizzy spells and Dickie's consultant told him to cut out the steroids. He advised me to do the same.

My doc came to the conclusion that Dickie was probably right. We followed the advice to 'kick 'em into touch'. That was years ago and I have never felt better.

Our picture shows Dickie at York races.

Dickie developed into a stylish and free-scoring batsman and he reached his peak with an innings of 181 not out for Yorkshire against Glamorgan at Bradford Park Avenue:

Fred was one of the first to give me a pat on the back. He said: "You've done your job well and now it's up to me" – and he was as good as his word. He was in top form. We won the game but my exhilaration didn't last long because I was dropped.

I wasn't told that I was dropped. Mr Sellars – and his committee of 42 selectors – just didn't pick me. I did play weeks later and made a few decent scores including an 89 and I finished the season with an average 48 which wasn't bad. But it became apparent that I had no future with the county side. I asked to be released three times by letter before they finally allowed me to go.

When I reflect on that decision to leave I regret having done so. Yorkshire cricket meant as much to me as it obviously did to Fred. But in those days we were simply minions and treated as such. I still have my first communication from Yorkshire CCC inviting me to Headingley. We were not regarded as 'Mister' or 'Sir'. One of my postcards reads: "Dear Bird. You will attend nets at 11 am. You will be paid ten shillings. JH Nash (Secretary)."

Everything was terse and to the point. We were servants of the club and under no illusions about our lowly standing. But I wish I hadn't left.

Dickie has countless memories of Fred and the cricket scene in general. He keeps in touch with the game's greatest – like Sir Garfield Sobers, who he rates as the best all-rounder ever to grace the world's cricket fields:

If you want to gauge Fred's standing in the history of our game have a word with Sir Garfield. He will tell you that Fred ranked with the best and was head and shoulders over many brilliant players. That tribute will do for me – and my dear friend Fred!

IAN BOTHAM

Cricket fans of advancing years will recall with a touch of nostalgia Fred Trueman at the peak of his prowess. They will remember that a silence descended on the scene when Trueman marked out his run-up before the opening over of either a Yorkshire or an England match, The hush was even more pronounced at Headingley where atmospherics often determined the flight and bounce of the ball in the action leading to the lunch break.

Similar quiescent anticipation ruled when Ian Botham – with bat in hand – embarked on an innings for his county or country. Cricket crowds expected fireworks from both charismatic players and were rarely disappointed. Fred invariably stated his intent with a vicious 'yorker' or a menacing bouncer much to the delight of the audience and the discomfort of the opposing batsman. Ian was a world-class all-rounder with swashbuckling employment of the bat and hostile swing bowling of varying pace. Like Trueman he played the game with never fading industry and enthusiasm.

Fred and Ian were 'peas in a pod' respectful of each other's contribution to cricket and able to make and take opinions and observations not entirely congratulatory. Fred was generous in praise of Ian's historic contribution to England's totally unexpected victory over Australia at Headingley in 1981. He also described Ian's autobiography as "phenomenal and standing out from an endless list of banal cricketing publications". Fred declared with justification that Ian was one player who could drag the drinking brigade from the cricket ground bars to watch him in action. It was high praise from Fred who is also on record as saying, "Ian couldn't bowl a hoop down a hill."

Ian once pointed out that Fred rarely had a good word to say about anyone who did not play the game in his day and he did not include him in his fantasy selection of cricketers to represent the 'Best of England'. Ian preferred Graham Dilley and Bob Willis in the role of pace bowlers. Despite the dropping of Fred from the 'make believe' team, Ian voiced admiration of the Yorkshireman's contribution to the game and his outspoken attitude when he believed he had an opinion to express.

It is a great pity that destiny and circumstances did not decree that Botham and Trueman played in the same era. They would have been a formidable duo against Australia, New Zealand, West Indies and the rest. Ian said: "It is a different game now and many people will not accept this truism. Fred would have been a good bowler in any era but he would not have the nickname Fiery."

Trueman and Botham had many things in common. They both played soccer. Ian was a pro with Scunthorpe United and Fred was on Lincoln City's books. Both were tireless workers for charity with Ian walking countless miles to secure over £4 million for research and treatment of leukaemia in children and Fred staging golf tournaments and other fund-raising events for the benefit of several notable causes. They were both summoned to Buckingham Palace to receive an OBE for their respective service to cricket and charity.

The present England side could certainly do with players of Trueman and Botham's magnitude. They were outstanding. Ian may well have been reflecting on past glories when he was tracked down in Australia during England's disastrous 2006 tour to give this assessment of Fred:

To every cricketer, Fred Trueman was the first superstar of the game. A great bowler – the first man ever to take 300 Test wickets – he was also a flamboyant, larger than life character. He didn't suffer fools gladly, always spoke his mind and stuck to his guns, no matter how many people disagreed with him; in some ways he was as rebellious during his playing career as I was in mine. And he was a ferocious competitor – if you played him at golf, he always had a problem counting!

At times he could be a very dour and tough character, but then the clouds would lift and he could be a great raconteur and entertainer. I remember doing a dinner with him in South Africa where we were meant to do twenty minutes each. I did three minutes, Fred did the other 37; we just couldn't get him off!

He'll be missed by me and a lot of other people, and certainly Radio 5 will never be the same without him. Whether he was right or wrong in what he said, didn't matter – Fred was Fred. The nearest we've got to him today is David Lloyd impersonating Fred. If there was ever a boring moment in play, 'Bumble' could always enliven it by doing his impersonation, and if you closed your eyes, you could be listening to Fred.

JOHN ARLOTT

When legendary Patsy Hendren retired from cricket he was asked for the reason behind his decision to quit the playing side of the game. Patsy replied: "Because I want to go while people still say 'Why?' and not stay until they say 'Why not?'"

This was probably behind Fred Trueman's decision to put away his bat, ball and pads at the age of thirty-seven, a move applauded by the superb cricket broadcaster and Fred's Test Match Special colleague, the late John Arlott:

It is generally agreed that no man remains a true fast bowler after the age of thirty. But Fred persevered and it would have been a tragedy if another season saw his bowling in severe decline. Such a fate would have cast a shadow over his magnificent career and his prominent role in cricket history.

Technically and imaginatively, Trueman was a great fast bowler. He first burst on the Test match scene in 1952. His debut gave all English cricket an uplift in morale that it had desperately needed since the 1939-1945 war. Ray Lindwall and Keith Miller had routed English cricket because our batsman had no experience of pace. England, ignominiously, had no power to reply. Then in 1952 the 21-year-old Trueman played his first Test match – against India at Leeds – and it was a sensational start to his international career.

It will always remain a mystery why he only played in sixty-seven of England's 120 Test matches between his first and last appearances. Yet he became the first bowler to take 300 Test wickets and ended his career with 307.

Fred was nearly six feet tall, wide shouldered with the broad stern, sturdy legs and strong feet a pace bowler needs. He surged up a belligerent long-curving run to a classic sideways-on delivery. He commanded the deadliest weapon of the fast bowler, the out-swinger which moves late from the line of the stumps. He bowled a bouncer as intimidating as his demeanour. He shocked and destroyed experienced players with the yorker.

In the Headingley Test of 1961 he destroyed Australia with 11 wickets for 88 in the match. In all he took 2,302 wickets in first class cricket. As a batsman of sharp eye and immense power he occasionally surprised with his high stroke making. He scored about 9,000 runs with three centuries. He made more than 400 catches, many of them at short leg where for many years he was quick, safe and brave.

His place in history is certain as a match-winning bowler. In the memory of all who have watched him, and even more of those who have known him, he remains the kind of character that, as some people complain, the modern game lacks.

Truculent, gregarious, histrionic – his appeals often seemed to be a dramatic end in themselves. He was voluble and violently anecdotal, sincerely, but at times exaggeratedly Yorkshire. He had the capacity to fill a stage, to charm or to infuriate.

Above all, as time refines recollection, we shall see him as a bowler, who, by fire, variety and a control of instinctive skill, defeated virtually all the best batsmen of his period, and at times simply shrugged aside those with slightly lesser powers.

English cricket will be the poorer for his going. It is improbable that the game will ever again know quite such another.

If you mentioned the name Neil Hawke to Fred, the Yorkshireman's face inevitably creased into a smile of remembrance and satisfaction. Mention Fred's name to Neil and he would respond with a rueful grin.

The Australian was Fred's world record 300th Test match victim at The Oval where the crowd erupted in a thunderous salute to his achievement. Neil was caught by Colin Cowdrey at first slip and was the first to congratulate the bowler, walking up the wicket, with hand outstretched, to shake hands with the remarkably cool Trueman.

Today, Fred would have been buried under a crowd of team mates after he had clenched his fist, punched the air and pointed rude signs at the Aussie players perched in the grandstand. But cricket triumphs were celebrated in dignified fashion in Fred's heyday and he reserved his joy for the evening when Neil and other Australian players joined the England internationals in a champagne toast to the man of the moment.

The ball that Fred employed on that momentous occasion was mounted and given a place of honour among Fred's collection of hard-earned trophies. He often recalled: "The 300th was the pinnacle of my bowling career and a lot of blood, sweat, toil and a few tears were shed in the years leading to that magical moment."

It probably rivalled the day he received his Yorkshire cap. This coveted item was buried in his father Alan's coffin.

JM KILBURN

JM 'Jim' Kilburn emerged from a grammar school education in Barnsley and a degree in economics secured at Sheffield University. A career in the wool business, or teaching, beckoned the tall, distinguished and rather handsome individual but he was a near fanatical cricket fan and he eventually found his niche in journalism.

Kilburn's byline became synonymous with classical and almost poetical summaries of cricket at county and international level. He cut an impressive figure. He was never one for chit-chat with juniors and, as a cub reporter, I was in awe of the man who walked the corridors of the Yorkshire Post home in Albion Street with a rather majestic gait. Such was his eminent standing that sub-editors were instructed, under pain of censure or even dismissal, never to tamper with JM Kilburn's copy. His words were almost as sacred as the bible. Deleting even a sentence was tantamount to sacrilege.

The edict not to change a word came from Yorkshire Post editor Arthur Mann who backed his judgment of the writer's brilliance by rewarding his work with the princely wage of £3 per week – a generous salary in 1934. Ten years later when my employment with the Yorkshire Evening Post started I was paid ten shillings for a five-and-a-half-day week with a twenty-five per cent war bonus taking my wage to twelve shillings and sixpence.

Kilburn's talent was worth every penny. His articles attracted universal appreciation with the established world cricket authority Neville Cardus congratulating the newcomer to the Press Box. When England routed India at Old Trafford, in 1952, his dramatic report reflected on the outstanding performance of FS Trueman:

Trueman did not bat in the second innings. Other business was in hand for him, beginning at half-past twelve. In nine overs he tore the frail Indian innings to shreds as a tiger would devastate a cage of canvas. He bowled as fast as any man has bowled at Old Trafford these twenty years and more, hurling himself into splendid and thrilling action with the allies of a following wind, a lively pitch, and indifferent light.

The exact measure of his quality can never be drawn because there was no experienced and sturdy batting against him. Some of it was dismissed without a chance to show mettle; the remainder was all too obviously without stomach for a fight.

Trueman's bowling was without technical, tactical, or moral reproach. All his victims save one were clean bowled or caught on the offside. Those who retreated with faint hearts towards square leg were as safe from injury as they were certain of cricketing ignominy. It was magnificent, pulse-stirring bowling, commanding the alternate silence and roar of the excited 25,000 who watched.

My favourite story of 'Jim' goes back to a match at Headingley when he sent a message to the office via a copytaker that there would not be any report for at least a couple of hours. The sub-editor waiting for the details of the game contacted his man-on-the-spot to ask why he would not be filing news and views etcetera.

Kilburn explained: "The grandstand is on fire."

The man in the office asked: "Have you contacted the news desk. Have you sent any details?"

Kilburn's reaction was: "I am here to report cricket . . . not fires."

His word was law. A young reporter was despatched to report on the possible conflagration.

JM Kilburn retired to his home in Harrogate. He was still a familiar impressive figure on the cricket circuit but had trouble with his eyesight. He was told by a specialist that his vision was perfectly safe. Six weeks later he was blind. His wife Mary then accompanied him to matches with her running commentaries enabling the cricket legend to maintain his passionate contact and interest in the game he and Trueman loved.

When Fred Trueman retired from county cricket, J.M. Kilburn wrote this evocative and outstanding assessment in the Yorkshire Post in November 1968:

No cricketer of modern times has made greater impact on public association with the game than FS Trueman. By his performances, by his behaviour, by his character he has printed himself indelibly on the cricket scene.

No one could deny him, no one would wish to deny him a place among the greatest of fast bowlers and he would have earned that place without reference to his statistical holdings. His 300 Test match wickets, his 1,700 wickets for Yorkshire are not a primary claim to remembrance. His bowling has been far more than his analyses.

Trueman has been a fast bowler by nature – by desire, by temperament, by the gifts of physical ability. He inherited strength of limb and co-ordination of muscular movement. He disciplined them into controlled power that developed into a superb and thrilling bowling action. The young Trueman, the untutored Trueman bowled with beauty.

From this basis, which was responsible for remarkable freedom from injury through a long career, Trueman set himself to learn, not bowling, but the art of first-class bowling. Maturity gave him strength, experience gave him authority. He was always a good bowler by the light of nature; thought for himself and generous assistance from others made him into a great bowler.

The young Trueman, called from military cricket to represent England, was seen in desperation one morning at Lord's. "Where can I find Bill Bowes?" was his urgent plea. Because he felt that only Bowes could solve the immediate problem of preventing the ball from swinging too much.

The very young Trueman and the ageing Trueman were helped by merciful restraint

JM Kilburn, whose cricketing articles attracted universal admiration.
In later life he became blind but still continued to attend matches.

from overwork. The Test match Trueman was fortunate in associates who increased his value by partnership. He learned, as all cricketers must, by living in cricket.

Step by step his abilities were augmented by knowledge. At the height of his powers when physical response and technical skill had been fused he was the complete fast-bowling force.

He could command the yorker and the bumper, outswinger and inswinger, variation of pace and he could raise inspiration from circumstances. Against the 1956 Australians at Lord's, Trueman epitomised himself to perfection. In an afternoon spell of bowling he held batsmen in thrall and spectators entranced with speed, swing, lift and sustained vigour that created an abiding cricket memory.

Trueman made visible, and sometimes audible, the attributes of fast bowling. His run-up was long and accelerating and at the delivery stride arms and legs were outstretched in the ideal 'cartwheel'. The back foot dragged sometimes, creating animosity, genuine or spurious, between umpire and bowler. Follow-through was smooth and sweeping.

Trueman revelled in his power. The slightest sign of fear in a batsman inevitably drew greater pace and probably shorter length. When he took eight wickets for thirty-one runs in an Old Trafford Test match, batsmen found his pace, increased by a strong following wind, no degree short of terrifying and some of the thirty-one runs were edged from a batting position discreetly near square leg.

The spirit that urged Trueman's most devastating bowling was not a technical affectation. Trueman was a volatile character of cricket. At times he bowled his bumpers misguidedly and at times he expressed his opinions forcefully and tactlessly. More than once he became a thorn in the side of administration and of cricketing goodwill.

He could be 'difficult', both on the field and off, but all through his career he invariably followed a moment of public disfavour with some dramatic and heart-warming performance as bowler or batsman or even in fielding. He could not avoid being a dramatic cricketer and there was little indication that he cared to be overlooked.

He marked out his run, rolled up a flapping shirtsleeve, tossed back an unruly lock of hair to create an effect. He let batsmen and all assembled know his opinion of the fortune of batsmen. He appealed with voice and gesture. He boasted and made good most of his assertions. He satisfied primitive urges in cricket; desires for conquest and its expression in terms of flying stumps.

He extended the same satisfactions into his batting, where his innings were expected to include a thumping six or a desperate attempt to achieve one. He was, in fact, a more accomplished batsman than he allowed himself to appear, but his public preferred him as a fast bowler taking his innings and Trueman became well aware of his public and of his own entertainment value.

Trueman as a cricketer won the admiration of two publics. He showed the comparatively simple-minded the elements of contest, the vigour, the breath-catching thrill. He revealed to the more studious and sophisticated a rare mastery of the subtler features of his art.

In all his cricket career, from the first overs at Cambridge to the day when he was left out of the Yorkshire team on grounds of loss of form, F.S. Trueman was never a nonentity.

HARVEY SMITH

Farmer, racehorse trainer, former international rider and archetypal Yorkshireman Harvey Smith was one of Fred Trueman's friends,

It was in 1958 when Harvey made his first indelible mark on the show-jumping world with victory on a little-known horse Farmer's Boy. From that humble start he soared to stardom on the domestic, European and, eventually, world scene.

His fighting spirit, no holds barred, and outspoken opinions – coupled with the occasional 'Harvey Smith' – gained him notoriety and a huge following of fans. The V-sign was once the preserve of Winston Churchill but, having been delivered a couple of times at members of show-jumping's nobility, it quickly inherited the Harvey tag.

Fred and Harvey are often likened to 'two peas in a pod' but Harvey disputes the theory:

We had much in common. We called a spade a shovel. Fred occasionally visited my stables but I am reminded of one of my old mother's sayings. She never tired of trotting out the advice: "Always be an individual and never be a copy."

Fred and I were individuals but had three things in common. We were born in Yorkshire. We were never reluctant to express our views. And we were winners. When Fred picked up the cricket ball he thought of nothing else but victory. He never entertained thoughts of defeat. I was exactly the same.

Fred was the best fast bowler in his era and I was top of the tree in my chosen sport. But there comes a time when one has to give way to up-and-coming youngsters. And it can hurt.

Fred was an amazing man and in his days bowled more overs than present day players. He was superbly fit and kept his fine condition because he was active in a full programme of matches. Today, players have stretch fractures, sprains, and all sorts of aches and pains because they don't put in the same amount of graft.

Mind you I hate making comparisons. Folk who never saw Fred play will possibly rate Darren Gough as the greatest Yorkshire fast bowler we have seen for some time. It is akin to comparing Lester Piggott with Frankie Dettori. It is impossible to gauge their respective talents.

But I will tell you that if Fred and Darren had bowled in the same era Fred would have still been the devastating force. And for my money Piggott would have ridden Dettori off the track. But all that is sheer speculation and a matter of opinion.

Fred told the truth as he saw it and he would have made a fine captain of Yorkshire county cricket team. On the few occasions he was entrusted with the leadership he did a great job. Fred was like his old mate Brian Close with the maxim – 'if we can't win we will draw'. Defeat was never envisaged.

It is little short of amazing how many people are prepared to praise a chap when he has gone to meet his maker. Why didn't they express such sentiments when he was alive. Fred had no time for those who decry people and eulogise with praise and sympathy when they have gone. Fred was truthful and he always surprised me by his political beliefs. He was an ardent supporter of the Tory party and for the son of a miner this was rather a strange action. But he had his views and he adhered to them.

When Fred Trueman arrived at the Yorkshire nets as a youth with enormous bowling potential his batting left much to be desired. Purists shuddered at the sight of the young lad clubbing the ball with scant regard for elegance, refinement or direction.
But his improvement over the years eventually gained him the respect of even the game's top bowlers.

Fred the flogger matured into a stylish batsman, although he often had to sacrifice his wickets as a tail-ender looking for quick runs. Fred hit three centuries against top-class opposition but he also reflected on other performances with justifiable inner satisfaction.

The 1958 season was far from brilliant for Yorkshire but Fred topped the club's bowling averages with 107 wickets. Rain cost Yorkshire a month of action. Six fixtures were lost to the elements but Fred was busy in Test match service against New Zealand. Fred experienced a goodly share of success and never forgot his batting performance at The Oval where his cavalier approach to the bowlers thrilled the partisan crowd,

Fred recalled: "I was facing a leg spinner A.M. Moir. He was a bowler of great repute but I 'carted' him for three successive sixes. My final score was 39 not out. But I was at the crease for less than twenty minutes. That was my top score in the Test arena, although I had plenty of 'thirties' to my credit.

"For Yorkshire I hit two centuries, one against Middlesex, at Scarborough, and one away at Northampton. My third was a hundred not out for an England team at Scarborough. I was very proud of that knock. It was my highest score in top class cricket."

Yorkshire folk – and many opposing fans – expected fireworks when Fred walked to the crease and he rarely disappointed them. He hit twenty-six half-centuries for the county and shared in several century partnerships - one with Brian Close at Northampton with his 104 topped by Brian's 161.

Fred said: "I enjoyed batting. I probably could have done better but I would never have approached Len Hutton's class. I could have watched him all day and often did. He was the best batsman I ever saw and it was a privilege to join him at the crease.

We batted together against Gloucestershire and they did their best to get me to the striker's end so they could bowl me out and finish the innings. But Len protected me. The opposition even gave him the chance off an easy four with the last delivery of one over. Len shouted: 'Just run three. It can't get to the boundary.' It didn't and Len retained the strike and he went on to make a century. I simply watched him with admiration."

Harvey Smith's busy schedule in the show jumping world denied him the opportunity to spend hours watching live cricket. He said: "I love all sports and cricket in particular. But most of my viewing was on television as opposed to visiting Headingley, Bramall Lane, and Park Avenue. I watched Fred from afar and admired his aggression, general attitude and his determination to win. I support competitors who never entertain losing and Fred was one of them."

Harvey faced many challenges in his chosen sport – not the least the invitation to correct the wayward antics of a celebrated horse called Hill House. This racehorse made headlines when it was discovered that he 'manufactured his own dope'. Something in his make-up and bloodstream gave positive results and he did not always tackle hurdles and fences with athletic alacrity.

Harvey said: "When I've finished with him he'll jump the Berlin Wall."

Harvey's approach to horses mirrored Fred's attitude to cricket. They both subscribed to the vow: "Never lose heart or give up."

When Fred was interviewed by Australian newspaperman Arthur Mailey he asked the Yorkshireman about his approach to forthcoming Test matches.

Fred replied: "If I'm picked to play against the Aussies I'll bowl like hell. If I hit 'em it will be too bad. But while I'm supposed to be a fast bowler I'm going to try and bowl fast. You can tell that to your papers out in Australia. The Aussies have got it to come."

BILL PERTWEE

Bill Pertwee enjoyed a friendship with Fred Trueman on a par with the affection he harbours for his alter ego Mr Hodges of everlasting Dad's Army fame. Bill also has a passion for cricket and he played to such a high standard he was expecting an invitation for trials with Essex. Fate declared that he would not further his sporting excellence at county level but he continued to turn out in club and charity games and made regular appearances with the Lord's Taverners.

Bill's life story, before his association with Fred, is an absorbing chronicle of jobs galore before he found his niche in the world of entertainment. He was a teenager when he was invited to work at the London Stock Exchange where he had a decent wage but quite a boring occupation. He was still waiting for the summons to Essex CCC from the legendary TN Pearce when he opted for an alternative career – cleaning windows.

So adept did Bill become at this work that he was promoted to an executive position with the company leading a team of window washers in the capital and Midlands. He had climbed the ladders to success – lots of them – when another career beckoned and, although he still had fingers crossed for the Essex invite, he plumped for the stage and the footlights.

Bill has fond memories of Leeds. He played pantomime at the City Varieties with Roy Hudd in 1959. He recalls life in theatrical digs and one particular dwelling in Roundhay, where he was welcomed by the landlady who gave him a tour of the premises.

She said: "We have two toilets – one downstairs and one upstairs. Please – NO SOLIDS – in the one at ground level."

Bill recalls: "I was once in a bit of a rush and had to pop in the downstairs loo and to my horror couldn't get the chain to work. I informed the landlady who said: 'Mr Pertwee - you have to surprise the chain. Pretend you are walking away then turn and pull sharply.' It worked."

Bill was in regular work in theatres and television when he gained the role of the irascible air-raid warden in Dad's Army. One episode featured Fred who was cast as Ernie Egan – a professional bowler in Mr Hodges' cricket team playing against a side skippered by the pompous Captain Mainwaring.

Fred enjoyed taking part in one of TV's enduring comedy series and the experience strengthened his friendship with Bill. During filming of that feature the cast and behind-the-scenes workers were invited to a wine promotion hosted by Colman's Mustard:

We were promised food as well as wine and we set off in a coach. Unfortunately all the food had been eaten by the time we arrived and so we wined on empty stomachs with the obvious result. Arthur Lowe, of Captain Mainwaring fame, started a singsong with Fred and then they both told several jokes – many of them a little ribald but very, very funny. This continued on the return journey and Fred suggested that we look for a fish and chip shop. We found one in a village and Arthur walked in and ordered 'forty cod and chips please'.

The startled proprietor said: 'I can't do forty.'

Arthur commanded: 'Do the best you can, man.' And he did,

We eventually returned to our hotel where we were expected to learn our scripts and prepare for the following day's filming. But Fred and Arthur's jokes continued into the early hours. Fred's memory for gags and his memory for cricket facts and sporting incidents was superb. He was an amazing man.

I admired him on Test Match Special and so did the late John Arlott. Fred didn't pull any verbal punches He spoke his mind and expressed opinions as he saw it.

Fred was also a very hospitable host to my wife Marion. We spent time with him and Veronica in the Dales. We love that beautiful part of the country. I have a senior citizen's rail pass and managed to get to Skipton via Leeds from King's Cross much cheaper than Fred could do it. He never got over the fact. He was a true Yorkshireman.

I also remember being with him at a Test Match at Headingley where one of the guests was TN Pierce, who often recruited teams to play at Scarborough Cricket Festival. I reminded him that I am still waiting for my trial for Essex. Alas it never came. But perhaps at the age of eighty I am just a wee bit too old for the first team.

I rang Fred about ten days before he died. He seemed to be in great form and quite confident about a recovery. Sadly he didn't make it and I lost a wonderful friend. I will never forget him or our outings to Bolton Abbey and meals at the Devonshire Arms. He was a good friend, a true pal, and one of the greatest of all cricketers. Bless him!

Bill Pertwee has fond memories of a night he was invited by Fred to a tribute dinner held in honour of his England colleague Brian Statham. He also recalls with more than a touch of nostalgia his visits to a couple of dinners at Sheffield Cricket Lovers' Society. These resulted in a meeting with the late John Arlott and a few drinks at The Crucible where championship snooker was taking place.

"What are you doing tomorrow?" asked John,

"Going home," replied Bill.

But Bill was tempted to visit Headingley and Brett's famous fish and chip shop where he was entertained to non-stop cricket memories over lunch with Fred's one-time mentor Bill Bowes.

Bill said: "Mr Bowes talked about the infamous bodyline Tests and we ate fine fish and chips and drank copious amounts of red wine. In fact we ran out of wine and John Arlott had to send his driver for more supplies. By the time I was on the train to London I didn't know whether I was on foot or horseback."

ROBERT LEDER

Bob Leder and Fred Trueman enjoyed a unique bond in as much as the man from New York had no feeling for cricket – except boredom – and his great chum was a legend in the game.

Bob was a 'big cheese' in New York. He was President of a motion picture company. He was also sales director for NBC and grew up with the likes of Mel Brooks and Woody Allen. Bob was in charge of three television centres – one concentrating on sport – and he later became President of the world renowned RKO.

Bob was a regular visitor to Fred's bedside during his final illness and has cherished memories of the friendship spawned in the heart of the picturesque Yorkshire Dales.

He is a keen racegoer. He owned horses in America and England. His Turf activities were blessed with minor success and he maintains a daily interest, speculating a few pounds on the outcome of races in all parts of Britain:

My stakes would not keep a bookmaker in cigars. They are very moderate and quite successful. Freddie would never gamble for the simple reason he never had cash on him. I remember the pair of us taking a taxi in New York to the Meadowlands and Freddie never paid his share. But I forgive him.

We were together on a memorable holiday in Sydney to watch the West Indies tackle Australia in a Test series. We wined and dined in great style, played golf, and met the likes of Richie Benaud and other cricketing heroes. We watched the Hobart boat race from a window in our hotel and had a truly marvellous time. It was a real ball because Freddie had friends wherever he went and he was so easily recognised.

I remember strolling with him in London and people just stopped and stared. Strangers were known to shout "Hi Fred" and I will tell you something I think is most significant in this celebrity-conscious world of ours. We have a lot of phoneys like those from Big Brother who become notable overnight and we have so-called musical stars with kids yelling for autographs. But I never saw anyone ask Fred for his signature. People wanted to stop and talk to him. They didn't clamour for his autograph. He appeared to be part of their family and this was characteristic of him and portrayed the deep affection the public reserved for this sporting hero.

He was truly a giant and the man in the street viewed him with great esteem. People felt that they could be personal with him, ask about his family and tell him about their offspring. Fred never treated it as an intrusion. I was in Piccadilly when a cabby stopped with four people in the back. He shouted "Hi Fred" and wanted a few words with him much to the bewilderment of the passengers who were paying the fare.

Fred enjoyed his status and meeting folk. I think he was unique in the world of athletes and so unlike today's super stars, who are protected by minders and body-guards. Fred was a true man of the people. If he had been born in my country he would have been in the same bracket of mega-stars and heroes like the baseball players Babe Ruth and Joe DiMaggio. Fred would have been revered and given the full film star treatment. Fred was not unknown in America. He appeared in cricket gear on Budweizer adverts and he was recognised by thousands.

Fred did not always have the press coverage he deserved. I'm afraid that in Britain the media build up heroes only to knock them down. Fred never actually received the accolades he deserved.

He had his human failings, which once impinged on his family life. But the likes of Babe Ruth and DiMagio had infinitely more sensational and well-recorded scandals than Fred who was soon back on track to enjoy the love of his family and delight in the Dales existence he discovered nearly four decades ago. Fred's obituaries were very kind. They stressed his regard for people of all walks of life and he remains a legend.

When I reached my sixtieth birthday Fred threw a party at his house. I was on my feet to say a few words and I had a fork in my hand with which I tapped the table to emphasise a point or two. It turned out that I scored and marked the table which was worth quite a lot of money. Fred didn't say anything on the night but he didn't talk to me for a month or so because I had damaged his property.

There was a time when he invited many cricket types and colleagues to parties. But that changed. He concentrated his invitations on family members, neighbours and friends. Broadcaster, author and journalist Don Mosey and solicitor Jack Mewies were always welcome.

I never saw Fred drink to excess. But I do recall him and Rugby Union great John Spencer introducing me to pints of Yorkshire beer and encouraging me to drink eight. Fred announced to all and sundry that I had achieved a record for an American but pointed out it was nothing for some of John's colleagues to knock back twice as much as I managed.

Fred loved the Dales more than socialising. He had a tremendous fondness for birds, wildlife, his dogs, other animals and the majestic scenery. But we occasionally deserted home for a visit to cricket matches. Fred often provided me with tickets even for Tests but I never really took to the game. I remember surviving one Test for a couple of hours before quitting my seat which probably cost somewhere in the region of a hundred pounds.

I grew up with celebrities and I am more sensitive to people who have that status than the man in the street. I also realise the attitude press people have to such persons because I was a journalist in the mid sixties and many celebs worked with and for me. Fred did not know he was a celebrity. He was a very normal guy. He had a fresh side and at times could be a little sarcastic. But he was always approachable and understanding. He had a huge charitable side, which helped worthy causes, and he did not court publicity.

One of my most vivid memories was of a near miss on a road in Spain. We were almost involved in a head-on crash as we travelled to play a golf game with Tony Jacklin. We missed disaster by inches. The other car was on the wrong side and we would definitely have been killed but for our timely swerve.

This incident brought us together and I will miss Fred – my dear friend. He was a big figure in my life and the circumstances of his passing were tragic in as much as we believed he was recovering. Veronica was at his side hour after hour and she asked me to visit because "Fred gets a kick out of you." He opened his eyes. Fred had lost his hair with the chemo treatment and I offered to take along a toupée I wore years ago.

Fred was tired but he laughed. After twenty minutes or more it was time for me to leave Veronica at his bedside. I thought he was on the mend and I was shocked when the news came that he had died.

He was larger than life. There are lots of celebrities who do not radiate. But he did.

I played a lot of golf with Arnold Palmer and other great players. So I knew where Fred fitted in life. He was not a glamour boy. He had simple tastes. He was – I repeat – a man of the people.

Fred Trueman enjoyed a pint or three of beer, but was also fond of 'bottled bubbly'. If there is anything he liked more than one bottle of champagne it was a handful! One of his many business roles included representing a champagne company, which he did with due respect for the firm's fine product. Fred is pictured at his Spanish home with the intention of introducing guests to the heady delights of 'champers'.

Said by Fred...

"Women are for batsmen, beer is for the bowlers. God help the all-rounders."

"I'd have looked even faster in colour." (said after watching himself on black and white television)

"The difference between a fast bowler and a good fast bowler is not extra muscle but extra brains."

"We didn't have any metaphors in my day. We didn't beat about the bush."

"I am here to propose a toast to the sportswriters. It's up to you whether you stand up or not."

"Use every weapon within the rules and stretch the rules to breaking point."

"If there is any game in the world that attracts the half-baked theorists more than cricket I have yet to hear of it."

"People started calling me 'Fiery' because 'Fiery' rhymes with 'Fred' just like 'Typhoon' rhymes with 'Tyson'."

"He is doing the best he can do. He's making the worst of a bad job."

"Fast bowling isn't hard work. It's horse work."

"Unless something happens that we can't predict I don't think a lot will happen."

"Anyone foolish enough to predict the outcome of this match is simply foolish."

Part 2

Bowled Over!

Fred Trueman's Cricketing Life

'FIERY FRED'

It was difficult to know when cricket legend turned sports journalist Bill Bowes was excited. It required a discovery of unbelievable impact to even wrinkle his imperturbable demeanour and equally serene brow. Bill returned from years in a German concentration camp to resume his cricket career with Yorkshire and when he finally stowed away his bat and ball he covered the scene for the Yorkshire Evening News. When that popular daily closed Bill strode a couple of hundred yards from Trinity Street, Leeds, to the Yorkshire Evening Post in Albion Street. It was there he succeeded cricket writer John Bapty in covering the Yorkshire games and also the Test matches.

Bill was allowed to spend time coaching aspiring young cricketers in the Yorkshire nets and one afternoon he returned to the office with a look of shell shock on his normally placid face. When Bill recovered his composure he announced to all prepared to listen: "I have seen a lad at Headingley who will not only play for the county. One day he will bowl for England and he will be a revelation."

Bill was a gifted amateur magician and a member of the Magic Circle but he could not conjure up enough words to illustrate the young bowler's potential. Bill and his coaching colleague Arthur Mitchell played roles of paramount importance in the development of this burgeoning star.

Bill said: "Fred Trueman's delivery swing is near perfection. Pace and control will follow. Everything has to be built around this natural swing."

Fred had immense regard for his tutors and you can imagine the astonishment of pedestrians who witnessed the unlikely scenario of Bill putting his protégé to work in the middle of Leeds town centre. Fred had called to see Bill at the Yorkshire Evening Post offices. The teenager felt he had a kink in his run-up and Bill left his typewriter unattended to take Fred outside and help him iron out the flaw.

Bill's prediction that Fred would eventually play for England materialised a few years later and it was John Bapty who rang the Royal Air Force Station, Hemswell, Lincolnshire, to break the news to Aircraftsman First Class Frederick Trueman that he had been selected to make his international debut. Fred was on National Service duty at the time and he had just returned to his duties at Hemswell after impressing selectors in a drawn game between Yorkshire and the old enemy Lancashire. He was busy catching up on work at the station stores when the call came to inform him that he would be required to play for England against India at Headingley.

Fred's reply to the "obvious hoax telephone message" was abrupt and not the sort of word one associated with a lad who often visited church twice on Sundays and was indeed an avowed Christian. John Bapty failed to convince Fred of the selection and he asked his colleague Bill Bowes to have a word with the dubious cricketer.

Fred recognised the voice of his former coach and there was unbridled elation when the news sank in that he had actually been picked to represent his country at the ground he regarded as a second home. Fred's debut on the England front was sensational. It has been well documented how he exploded on the international scene and quickly earned the pseudonym 'Fiery Fred'.

Read Fred Trueman's memoirs and you will discover that he was a 'bit of an imp' as a child. So it was probably appropriate that his soccer adventures took him to sign for the 'Imps' – Lincoln City.

Fred played football for RAF Hemswell when he was engaged in two years' National Service. He said: "I was a 'bustling centre-forward' and turned out as an amateur for the City second team. Later the manager Bill Anderson wanted me to turn professional but it was feared by Yorkshire Cricket Committee that I could pick up serious injuries and this could affect my cricket career. I had to turn down the invitation and the money that went with the proposed contract."

Fred occasionally pulled on his soccer boots for amateur and charity matches but thankfully he did not play in a one heated encounter between Yorkshire CCC players and a team formed from Leeds United's side of all talents. In that game the late wicket keeper David Bairstow and Raymond Illingworth were the targets for that tough little hard man Bobby Collins.

Bobby kicked David and Raymond from pillar to post and if Fred had been on the receiving end his own brand of 'bustling' would have come into play and possibly wreaked havoc.

Bobby was warned with the message: "Take it easy. It's only a friendly."

The wee Scot replied: "There is no such thing in football."

This picture shows Fred soaring to head the ball watched by 8,500 Lincoln supporters. Fred said: "I enjoyed the sport but cricket was my real love – and my job."

Another employee of the Yorkshire Evening Post, photographer Harry Fletcher, captured pictures of the young man in action. He produced prints of the bowler's victims and a snap of the scoreboard showing the visitors in deep trouble. I helped Harry to caption the photographs. They were sent to Fred and our friendship – cemented on that occasion – continued until my favourite cricketer's untimely departure at the age of 75.

I was born twelve months before Fred. I was also the son of a miner. I did my National Service at Hemswell and was posted to Egypt for eighteen months. When I arrived at Hemswell I was asked by the reception officer if I had any interest in sport. My reply was "horse-racing" and his sarcastic reaction was: "We will build a track for you at the back of the cookhouse."

He must have rubbed his hands with glee when Fred arrived and told him he was a cricketer. There was no question of this recruit leaving a station where the game was played to a high standard.

Fred represented the RAF against the Army and the Navy. You can guess the results. Fred's figures were very impressive.

EARLY DAYS

On one occasion Fred and his playing colleagues signed into a Portsmouth hotel the evening before the start of a match with Hampshire.

Fred said: "I had a lovely room. It overlooked the Solent and I remember spending half an hour or so watching a submarine at exercise. Frank Lowson, Roy Booth and me strolled into town for a meal and I returned about ten o'clock to have an early night. I opened the door and fast asleep in my huge double bed was Herbert Walker – our club scorer.

"I shook him and asked for an explanation. He simply rolled over and murmured that he was sharing with me. I was furious and yelled that there was no way I would share a bed with him. Herbert's response was 'you don't have to – there's a put-you-up in the bathroom'. This was the limit. The club's star bowler was expected to sleep in a bathroom and the scorer was given the luxury of a huge bed."

The following morning Herbert woke Fred because he needed the toilet. Fred complained to the skipper but there was nothing Norman Yardley could do about the situation.

Fred added: "That is how first team players were treated in the 1950s and the early

1960s. We were expected to take the rough with the smooth and be satisfied with the privilege of playing for Yorkshire.

He continued: "When I look back on those days I realise that it was our loyalty to the county, our sheer determination and our pride in playing for Yorkshire which carried us to so many victories. We soon forgot the little things that irked, like giving up a bed to the scorer, although we knew that similar treatment was not meted out to players in other counties.

"When I first played for Yorkshire the situation was that if you got a second team cap you would walk into any other county's first team. If you secured a Yorkshire first team cap you realised that it was a great honour not only for yourself but for the rest of the family. Even remote uncles, aunties and cousins basked in reflected glory.

"What it means today is unknown to me. To play cricket for Yorkshire was the pinnacle of my lifetime. It was a great achievement because you had to earn the cap. They were not given lightly. One had to measure up to standard to gain the accolade.

"However you had to live up to the honour. The crowd certainly let you know if your ability slipped. Yorkshire fans knew the game. They were great spectators – especially those at Bramall Lane, Sheffield. The South Yorkshire lads and lasses certainly enjoyed cricket and soon spotted a non-trier. They would be the first to let you know their feelings and you listened to remarks like: 'You played well' or 'You bowled like a twat.'

"The Bramall Lane spectators were always free with praise or criticism and it was a crying disgrace when the ground closed. It was sad for me because that is where I started my professional career.

"Of course my amateur introduction to the game started when I was about six and we played our matches in a field liberally sprinkled with cow pats. When the cows were removed for Saturday matches two notices were pinned to the wall of our changing room. One read: 'If the ball has landed in a cow pat it must be rolled to the wicket keeper and not thrown.' The other asked: 'Those responsible for making the tea and sandwiches are asked to leave the pitch early so they can wash their hands before serving our visitors.'"

The Trueman career was given an early start and little did Fred know in those far-off days that he would eventually play for Yorkshire and England.

Fred signs his autograph for a small schoolgirl on the occasion when he was awarded the Freedom of Maltby. It meant as much to him as the Keys of the Kingdom as it was "given by true friends and honest people" in the South Yorkshire community where he went to school.

NO BALL!

Fred had a great regard for Yorkshire wicket-keeper Jimmy Binks and often reminded any official and selector prepared to listen that this brilliant stumper deserved more England caps that the two he received.

Fred said: "Jimmy was sheer class behind the wickets. It was a crime that he was not called up for international duty more often."

Yorkshire usually played a pre-season match at Ampleforth where the college boasted players of a truly high standard. Before one game Fred and Jimmy hit on a plot to bring a little light relief to the encounter and – at the same time – strike terror into the opening batsman.

Fred welcomed the first two on the field with the barely concealed whisper: "I feel great and ready for action. I'll be bowling off my long run."

This threat was sufficient to strike fear into the bravest heart and Fred hollered to Jimmy: "Stand well back. I'm in a rare mood."

If the young Ampleforth student, preparing to face Fiery Fred wasn't already a nervous wreck, he certainly was when he saw Fred retreating almost to the boundary line before turning to embark on his run-up. What the batsman did not know was that Fred didn't have a ball in his hand. It was in his pocket.

Fred accelerated into that majestic, side-on, approach, gathering momentum and finally delivering nothing but following through with a mighty shout. Jimmy slapped his gloves together and the packed slip fielders leaped and shouted in unison "Howzat!"

The quaking batsman saw the umpire's finger raised and he prepared to walk back to the pavilion with the remark: "I never even saw the ball."

It was then Fred's face took on a beaming grin as he halted the departing batsman and explained what had taken place.

Fred recalled: "He took a lot of convincing. He didn't want to return to the crease. But eventually he did and I went back to my short run. They were happy days. My old pal Don Wilson, of Yorkshire and England fame, is one of the coaches at Ampleforth and I do believe that the actor Peter O'Toole helps out when he is resting."

The famous picture was taken by the late Yorkshire Post photographer Harry Fletcher, who presented Fred with photographs of his explosive start to his international career.

Fred burst on the Test match scene at Headingley in 1952. He was in the RAF and was given leave of absence by his Group Captain Jim Warfield, who congratulated the Yorkshireman on his elevation to the England side.

England opposed India and Fred collected his first Test wicket when Polly Umrigar edged a Trueman delivery into the gloves of wicket-keeper Godfrey Evans. Fred finished the first innings with three wickets and was delighted that he had achieved the feat in front of a partisan Yorkshire crowd. India made 293 and England replied with 334 for nine declared.

Then Trueman struck with a vengeance. He was successful in his first over with Pankaj Roy caught by Denis Compton. In the second over Alec Bedser took Gaekwar's wicket caught by Jim Laker. Two Trueman wickets followed with Mantri's middle stump flying before Manjrekar's wickets cartwheeled. And the scoreboard read four for none. This unique picture went round the world. Never before or since has such a Test scoreboard registered such a bowling achievement

Fred's dad Alan was in the crowd no doubt sharing his son's triumph and sub-editors were ringing cricket reporters to verify the figures. India eventually rallied and England had to bat again with a mere eighteen runs required for a comprehensive victory.

Fred's career finished with a Test record of 307 wickers and it would have possibly been 500 had circumstances not conspired to deprive him of another thirty or forty international matches or more.

Fred with his great friend and England colleague Brian Statham. They formed a world-renowned opening partnership. Fred's nickname for Statham was 'George' and he sometimes addressed him as 'Kangaroo'.

Their performances for England suggested they were 'joined at the hip' but mutual favours did not exist in any Roses Match when Fred played for his beloved Yorkshire and Brian boasted fervent loyalty to Lancashire. Fred was a great admirer of Brian's spot-on accuracy with the ball and Brian envied his mate's ability to swing the ball at will. They were a powerful duo and the sort the current England side needs.

HOLY ORDERS

There was a time when Fred – tongue in cheek – vowed he would take 'Holy Orders' and retire to the silence and privacy of a monastery. He explained: "It was the only escape route from the rubbish spoken and written about my suspect behaviour, drinking and bacchanalian lifestyle."

Fred often recalled an occasion when he had to ask the Yorkshire County Cricket Club physio Bright Heyhurst for treatment to his back and legs. Bright took his pipe from his mouth and said: "Anyone who crawls into a hotel at 4.30 am doesn't deserve a rub down."

Fred said: "Our skipper Norman Yardley overheard the physio and demanded an explanation."

Bright replied: "I was talking to the night porter at half-past four this morning and Trueman, Frank Lowson, and Roy Booth were still out. It's a disgrace."

Norman asked: "Is this true Fred?"

"No it is not," said Fred "We had a pint in the hotel bar and were in bed no later than 11.30pm."

Bright insisted: "No you were not. The night porter can verify that you and the others were not here."

Frank Lowson and Roy Booth chimed in with: "Fred's right. We were tucked up in bed well before midnight."

Norman asked Bright: "Which hotel are you staying in?."

He answered: "The Denmark."

Norman asked: "Where are you booked in Fred?"

He replied: "Snows – with Frank and Roy."

Fred recalled: "Bright's face was a picture, but we didn't get an apology."

Over the years Fred had to issue denials of many false stories, which collected credence and momentum with repetitive telling of the totally fictitious tales. One disturbing falsehood cited his "disgusting behaviour and bad language" at a Bristol Hotel where the Yorkshire team stayed during a match with Gloucestershire. Fred had to appear before the Yorkshire committee to explain his conduct.

He said: "I don't know how I happened to be in two places at once. However, I was not in Bristol. I was playing for England at Lords at the time I was supposed to be swearing at a hotel I have never even visited."

He was also accused of similar bad behaviour in a Worksop hotel and 'banned from the premises for life'. Fred had never been to the hotel but decided to call in to clear his name. The landlady who made the complaint didn't even recognise him.

Fred said: "I am sure there was one or even more blokes pretending to be me."

He was once asked to apologise for his drunken antics at the Queens Hotel, Leeds. He was playing for Yorkshire in Brighton at the time.

He said: "Believe me, I was one of the most sober men in county cricket. I was not in the first three leagues when it came to knocking back pints but stories persisted that I was a seasoned boozer. My career as a fast bowler would have collapsed if I had supped to excess."

Fred added: "God only knows what some folk were saying. That is why I suggested taking Holy Orders and spending the rest of my days in a monastery."

When Fred lapsed into nostalgia mode his recollections stretched from hilarious to emotional. His memories were prodigious and defied contradiction. He had total recall of the most minimal incidents and his detailed remembrance of major achievements was treated with respect and admiration. In short he had a superb memory for facts both startling and frivolous. You didn't argue with Fred. Even Methuselah took a back seat.

One of Fred's greatest cricketing friends was the brilliant England, Gloucestershire and Worcestershire batsman Tom Graveney. Tom was one of the guests at the annual Len Hutton 364 Luncheon at Headingley a couple of years ago when he teamed up with his old England colleague Fred. The pair reminisced at great length and dwelt on Graveney's performance against the West Indies in 1957 when Tom hit a glorious 258 at Trent Bridge.

Fred recalled more details of that momentous display than Tom who was summoned back to the England Test side in 1966 at the age of 39. He played for his country for another three years and – like Fred – he was awarded the OBE. It was Fred who mentioned the fact that the Queen addressed Tom as "Mr Gravy". Tom had forgotten that royal slip of the tongue. But Fred hadn't.

Our picture shows Tom (left) with Humberside captain Brian Roper, Fred Trueman, and another England batsman – the silver-haired David Steele. Fred's nickname for David was 'Crime' because of his careful attitude to money.

Fred explained: "David was always thrifty and was never known to buy anyone a drink. He adhered to the claim that 'Crime does not pay' – hence his nickname."

Fred was delighted when his long time friend Tom Graveney was elected President of the MCC.

COMPELLING READING

When the late John Arlott penned his book *Fred* he was aware that the chosen subject would be a sporting bestseller – especially at £2 per book. Fred's career was in its twentieth turbulent season and the esteemed author and broadcaster knew that the Yorkshire cricketer's activities on and off the field made compelling reading. Arlott did not pull any punches and Fred had no complaints. He appreciated Arlott's friendship and admired his broadcasting skills and descriptive phrases.

Arlott could always summon an accurate comment on any incident. He was blessed with a rich vocabulary and an inspired selection of depictive expressions. However, the magic often deserted him late in the day when the lunchtime wine threatened his waking hours. There came a time when Arlott commentated in the hours before lunch and certainly not after the break for sustenance.

Fred particularly enjoyed Arlott's verbal contribution at Lords when a chap decided to undress and enter the arena. "We have a freaker," said Arlott (he'd mistaken the word for streaker). "Very shapely and it is masculine. I think he has seen the last of the cricket today which for him is to his detriment as a dramatic feast is beginning to unfold."

Arlott was also cool and unruffled with such memorable observation of a long and dogged innings by Geoffrey Boycott. The commentary finished with: "No man is an island but he has batted as though he was a particularly long peninsula."

Arlott was at times strong on Fred in the book, which carried the sportsman's name. He wrote "No cricketer since the war captured the public interest, or press headlines, with greater frequency than Yorkshire and England bowler Fred Trueman. He was a man of extremes. He was liked and disliked. He hated batsmen and showed his feelings with a bumper as vicious as can be imagined."

Arlott claimed: "Fred was a fast bowler in his mind and also in his heart. When the fire burned brightly he was as fine a fast bowler as has ever lived."

But the Trueman trait which really endeared him to Arlott was his wit and outspokenness. At a party in Aden, Fred was introduced to a sheik and one of the hosts said "He has 196 wives."

"Has he?" said Fred, "Does he know he can have a new ball with four more?"

Arlott recalled another occasion: "When Fred first played for Yorkshire in May 1949 the lad from Maltby was presented with a menu in French. He pointed to the date printed at the bottom, 'Jeudi le douzieme Mai', and said: 'Aye I'll have that for my sweet.'"

Arlott and Trueman enjoyed each other's company and the writer's favourite story refers to Fred's ability to tell tales often sprinkled with the kind of Anglo-Saxon that would shock the establishment but delight the majority of cricket fans. Much to Arlott's amusement, when a batsman had the temerity to swear at Fred he reported the incident to the umpires and they solemnly forwarded his complaint to Lord's.

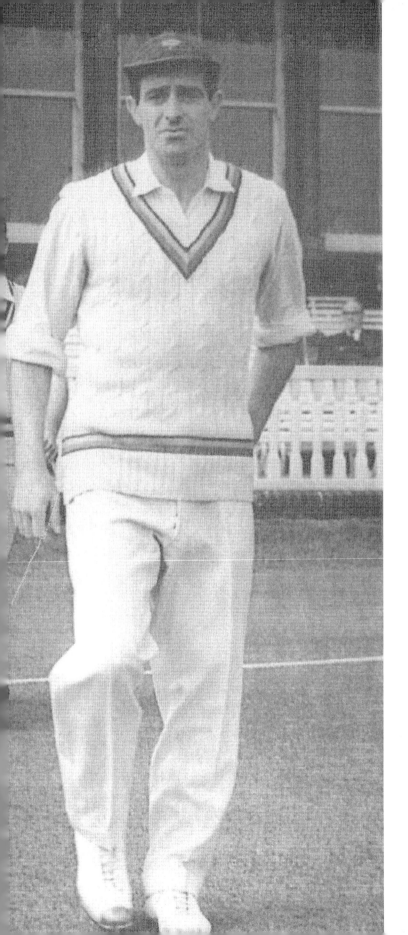

Fred leading out the players against the 'Gents'. In 1962 Fred was asked to captain the Players against the Gentlemen in the match that was the last in the long history of this fixture. The matches date back to 1806 and with only a couple of exceptions were staged at Lords.

Fred was deeply honoured to lead the professional players into action and, although rain forced the game to be drawn, he always cherished the fact that he had been elected skipper. He said: "When the matches were first played there were at least fifty or sixty amateurs in county sides. But the ranks of the unpaid brigade dwindled and the description 'amateur' was eventually dropped."

Fred would have loved to lead his team of players to victory. He recalled: "We were faced with a modest total to chase but the rain decided the outcome."

DAYS WITH DON MOSEY

Don Mosey was one of Fred Trueman's loyal friends and a working journalist who eventually found fame in television and as a gifted author. We were colleagues at the Yorkshire Evening Post where he blossomed as a brilliant reporter specialising in features and coverage of police courts from minor hearings to quarter sessions and vastly important Assizes. However, his thoughts often strayed to all things cricket. He was a gifted fast bowler of top league standard and he often entrusted his reporting assignments to colleagues and played truant to attend Headingley matches.

Typical of Don's writing was this piece on Fred, written just before he achieved his three hundredth Test wicket:

"Fred has never disliked publicity, so long as it was not the sort which just 'had a go at him' idly and irresponsibly. He has never really appreciated that as the world's greatest cricket personality – a title which he revels in – everything he does has a certain news value.

"He can be a good friend and a bad enemy, and he has never attempted at any stage of his life to avoid making enemies. He has scores of them.

"Through fifteen years of triumphant appeals and fearsome scowls, through ten thousand overs of sweat and effort, of dazzling success and failure, through one tidal wave after another of violent controversy, Trueman has remained the idol of the crowds and the scourge of batsmen."

Don was a regular supporter of the journalist watering holes – the Victoria, adjacent to Leeds Town Hall, and the ever-popular Whitelocks. He was a fiery bowler for the Yorkshire Evening Post departmental side with fellow reporter Frank Laws sharing the pace attack. They were great pals on and off the field. However, after one lengthy session at Whitelocks they squared up outside the pub to settle an argument.

I felt duty bound to intercede and stood between the two six-footers. They both threw wild punches, missing each other, but catching the unofficial referee – me – on the jaw. They then clutched each other in a friendly embrace and harmony was restored without any semblance of an apology to their damaged colleague.

When Don's first son was born we wet the baby's head to such a tune that the proud father was unable to visit his wife and offspring the same evening. He booked a room in the Queens Hotel, Leeds. The following day the 'hair of the dog' was a must and this resulted in more 'head wetting' and another night at the Queens Hotel. But he eventually reached home for a joyous union with his wife and offspring.

Don joined the Daily Mail and the newspaper staged an annual cricket match against the Daily Express. Australian star all-rounder Keith Miller was on the Express cricket-reporting staff. Such was the rivalry by the national papers that the Express felt justified in selecting Miller for the office team.

The Daily Mail responded by hiring a private plane to bring Don back from Ireland where he was writing an article on the Irish author and renowned drinker Brendan Behan. Don clean bowled Miller to justify the expense and the trip.

He later joined the BBC and was executive producer of outside broadcasts with a senior role on the much-loved Test Match Special. Don assured Fred that he would have a place in the TMS team for as long as he was associated with the programme. Don finished with the production in 2001 and Fred and his great mate Trevor Bailey were dropped on the same day after contributing to the success of the output for a couple of decades.

Fred often recalled: "We had little warning. I was in Spain and the Head of Sport telephoned to give me the news. He started by saying that he didn't really know how to speak to a sporting icon. But he did."

Fred and Don maintained their fervent friendship for years. Don was tall, elegant, slim and a great athlete. He was a good golfer, an excellent cricketer and a gifted journalist. It was a privilege to work with him.

'PUT YOUR HANDS TOGETHER'

Many quotes are attributed to Fred Trueman and repeated in print and conversation.
One concerns the Reverend David Sheppard who was not only a Church of England Bishop but an England international cricketer of great repute. After David had taken a catch it was reported that Fred said to his colleague: "Let's face it Rev when you put your hands together you have a better chance of catching than any of us."

Fred always denied that he was the instigator of the oft-quoted quip. But he does tell another story of Bishop David's fielding: "David was a fine batsman but his work in the field left a lot to be desired. We had first class catchers of the ball in our England teams but I'm afraid David was not one of them. We travelled to Australia for a tour and in matches building up to the first Test David had a nightmare in the field. He must have dropped a dozen catches. Some were 'dollies' and should have been caught by David with his eyes shut.

"The first Test arrived with 30,000 Aussie fans yelling for their heroes. It is an intimidating hullabaloo. They really get behind their players and give the English lads never-ending stick. The noise is deafening from the first ball to the close of play.
It was 1955. We were hell-bent on winning and when Brian Booth lifted a skier with David underneath we waited with sheer trepidation and confidence that he would drop it.

"But he didn't. He held on to the ball. He was so elated he tossed the ball high again and caught it. He repeated the celebration with 30,000 Aussie voices hollering – and the England lads yelling too: 'Throw the ball back to the bowler. Brian hit the catch from a no-ball. They've already run four!'

"He hadn't heard the call because of the noise and it was in that match I was supposed to have made reference to David 'putting his hands together'. The legend is quite untrue."

Fred added: "David was a wonderful man. He surrendered his brilliant cricket career for the cloth. He was not only a brilliant sportsman – he was also a great man of the church."

It is calculated that twenty-seven bowlers shared Yorkshire's opening attack with Fred – not the least Tony Nicholson (left) and Mike Cowan. Tony died at a very early age and Fred attended his funeral at Ripon Cathedral where he spoke with great affection for the man who - like David Sheppard - was a suspect fielder.

Fred said: "We often sent Tony as far from the wicket as possible. He fielded on the boundary and he had one great thing in his favour. He had a mighty arm and his throw-in to the keeper was always direct, stump-high and it saved many runs, in addition to contributing to run-outs.

Mike Cowan attended St Michael's College in Leeds. The school was also Alma Mater to Yorkshire's Brian Bolus and Frank McHugh. Mike lived in Doncaster and throughout his schooldays he caught the 7.25 am train to Leeds and he claims that he was never late for school.

Mike has a fund of stories and bases his after-dinner speeches on his cricketing life with Fred. He said: "I roomed with Fred for nine years. He was like a brother to me. He was the one who got me started on the speaking circuit and I will always be grateful to him for this encouragement. He was a great bowler and a wonderful man. We shared many happy hours."

SMART AND CLEAN

Fred deplored the way even England players dress today. He said: "In my days we wore the Yorkshire blazer with genuine pride. We were told to wear it on all occasions – even during the lunch period – on match days. We would come from the field, have a quick wash, comb our hair those who had any, and on with the blazer. We were under orders to be smart and I am all in favour of this edict.

"Players are not proud of their image today. I want to tell them but they would term me old-fashioned. And I don't mind being old-fashioned. We cleaned our shoes, pads and even our cricket bats. I see players today with filthy shoes and can't believe it. The game has changed and the modern attitude to smartness and cleanliness would not have happened in my day. The captain would have given me a rare rollicking

"Of course some have excuses on the grounds of superstition. One chap won't clean his bat because he fears he would wipe the runs away. What a load of nonsense!

"Mind you I had one superstition. When I was padding up to go into bat I always put my left pad on first. Don't ask me why! It was just a foible. I saw players with little figures in their pockets and lucky champagne corks in their bags. All these little good luck charms were in evidence. But we were clean – very clean. There is no excuse for being scruffy.

"The Yorkshire teams I knew were a credit to themselves, the game and Yorkshire. We were drawn from all parts of the county. We had different dialects. But we were a team and if we had any differences they were forgotten when we went on the field."

TWELFTH MAN

Chris Old was one of the twenty-seven bowlers to share Yorkshire's opening attack with Fred Trueman. He acquired the nickname 'Chilly' because of 'C.Old', which appeared on scoreboards. But he was certainly warm stuff when it came to batting and bowling.

Chris now resides in Penzance, Cornwall, where he has a thriving fish and chips restaurant and takeaway. But he still follows the fluctuating cricket fortunes of Yorkshire's county side and the England scene to which he gave so much with bat and ball.

Fred was his mentor and Chris was happy to learn from the man he was destined to replace in the county side and also on the international front.

Chris recalls: "When I joined Yorkshire I was known as a batsman. But I knew that Fred was coming to the end of his career so I decided to develop the bowling side of my game. Fred's boots were difficult to fill and I knew that even if I did take his place in the team I would never replace him as an icon."

Chris learned much from Fred and the other Yorkshire giants Brian Close and Ray Illingworth. When he was picked to take Fred's spot in a match against Warwickshire, at Middlesbrough, no one was prepared to tell Fred that he was twelfth man. The night before the match Fred was with a few journalists, including me, in the Swan and Talbot at Wetherby. Fred was in great form. He proceeded to tell anyone prepared to listen that he was going to win the forthcoming game single-handed. He felt great and couldn't wait to pin a few batsmen against the wall. I didn't have the nerve or temerity to show him the front page of the Yorkshire Evening Post, which stated: 'Trueman bombshell. He is dropped.'

Fred was truly hurt. He learned the news from the opposing captain Alan Smith. Yorkshire finished the season as champions but Fred was now coming to the end of his remarkable career and he began to contemplate retirement. It is doubtful if we will see his like again.

LOOKING BACK

Fred was offered the captaincy of Yorkshire two days after he had decided to end his career with the county. He had already written an article in the People newspaper to confirm his decision to retire from the game.

Fred recalled: "I knew there were certain members of the committee who would have enjoyed me being sacked but in a meeting with the club president, Sir William Worsley, I was told that discussions were taking place to make me skipper. I informed Sir William that if anyone had hinted to me about that possibility two days before I would have cancelled plans for my future. But there was no way I could stop the story going in the paper. The early editions were already off the press. So I missed being captain of Yorkshire by a few hours. It was an incident I regretted for the rest of my life."

I once talked to Darren Gough about Fred and naively asked him if he had modelled his action on Trueman. Darren admitted that he knew little about the man who preceded him as a great Yorkshire and England player. Darren said: "I had heard of him from other folk but never saw him play. My hero was Ian Botham."

Many of Fred's opinions were critical of other players but there were times when he believed praise was necessary. He said:

"Len Hutton was the greatest England batsman I had the honour to play with. But he caused me a bit of trouble on the West Indies tour when I came in for unfair criticism.

"Norman Yardley was too much of a gentleman to be a captain. He didn't have the iron hand with which to rule personalities like Hutton, Johnnie Wardle and Bob Appleyard.

"Billy Sutcliffe was a first class bloke. He would have made a good Yorkshire skipper if he had been given half a chance.

"Ronnie Burnet was a man of iron. If he wanted a thing doing it would be done. At the same time he could charm anybody and if you did well for him he would do well for you.

"Brian Close was brave and a great captain. He was fearless in the field and impervious to pain.

"Raymond Illingworth was one of the world's greatest all-rounders and a brilliant captain."

Of himself Fred said: "I should have been skipper. I was cut out for the job."

NEVER SHORT OF A WORD

Lancastrian David Lloyd was a member of the BBC's Test Match Special team and he enjoyed hours of repartee with his colleague Fred Trueman.

David recalls: "The most enjoyable times were when we had to fill the programme when rain curtailed play. It was then Fred came into his own. He could 'rabbit' for hours and to hear him talk he must have taken five million wickets and averaged over a thousand a week. Fred took the lot with middle-dolly yorkers. He never bowled a wide delivery. They were all unplayable and directly en route for the stumps. We loved his slight exaggeration."

David adds: "Fred was never short of a word or a thousand and one of my many vivid memories was the day he outlined to a startled colleague, Christopher Martin-Jenkins, the spartan days of outside toilets. Fred went into great detail and when Christopher described his own luxurious bathroom, equipped with a bidet, Fred interrupted with: "We have them in Yorkshire. But we call them flannels."

David reflected on the day the 'Free George Davis' clan desecrated the Headingley Test wicket with oil, tar and hatchets. Sir Len Hutton turned to Fred with tears in his eyes and murmured: "How could they . . . how could they?"

Fred was more outspoken. He growled: "I would grab those responsible and drop them head first from the top of the pavilion. Mind you, I would give them a chance and place Keith Fletcher underneath to catch them."

Keith was not known to have "a safe pair of hands"!

Sir Len Hutton, who was visibly distressed when the Headingley Test wicket was desecrated by 'Free George Davis' supporters.

Fred was proud of his long and dedicated service to Test Match Special and he is pictured at the centre of the team with Trevor Bailey on his right and Henry Blofeld (left) and the rest of the team looking on. Trevor was a great batsman and Henry 'Dear Old Thing' was one of the many colourful characters in this collection of cricket experts.

FAST BOWLERS

One of my last conversations with Fred dwelt on the present crop of fast bowlers and he posed a significant question. Fred asked: "Name the last recognised opening bowler to take a century of wickets for his county in a season?"

I ventured several names without success and was rather surprised with Fred's answer.

"It was me!" said Fred "And I did it for Yorkshire."

The statistic is staggering even taking into consideration that players do not play as many seasonal county matches as they did in Fred's halcyon days.

Fred said: "It is a disgrace. Fast bowlers today are not earning their wages on the county front."

A few weeks after our discussion I attended a cricket function at Brighouse where several dignitaries, including Dickie Bird, were in the audience. I decided to pose Fred's question and there was a barrage of wrong answers with Dickie responding with medium pace bowlers and even spinners. When I produced Fred's answer that he was the last fast bowler to achieve the feat he performed with regularity Dickie jumped to his feet and hollered: "I'm not having that. Fred's wrong."

My response was: "Well you go and tell him Dickie. Because I won't. It is not safe to contradict Fred. His knowledge of cricketing statistics is phenomenal."

If you check the record books you will see that Fred was telling the rather sad truth. We do not appear to have many Truemans – if any – in county cricket today.

Fred often alluded to this claim. He said: "With all due respect, cricket has not had a player to capture the imagination of the public or empty the bars at grounds since Ian Botham."

It was always unwise to contradict Fred so I refrained from putting Andrew Flintoff's name in the equation. Mind you, Fred once said of Ian Botham: "He couldn't bowl a hoop down a steep hill."

It was a balmy evening at Headingley. The sun was setting and play in a Test match had ceased for the day. Fred Trueman had finished a stint on Test Match Special and with pipe in hand he walked with fellow broadcaster Richie Benaud, ex-Aussie all-rounder Keith Miller, Rugby League star Arthur Clues and a much younger John Morgan to a marquee erected near the now defunct Bowling Green Club. Specially invited guests drank in the marquee and the approaching party of five invaders was intercepted by a uniformed attendant..

"Sorry sirs," he said, "Only gentlemen with passes can enter."

"Quite right too," replied Fred, "Keep the riff raff out."

The startled commissionaire had no response to Fred's attitude and he allowed us to pass into the scene of unbridled alcoholic celebration. At one point, Fred volunteered to help the busy staff to cope with the privileged drinkers.

Keith Milller was one of the greatest Australian cricketers and he shared a brilliant partnership with Ray Lindwall. When Keith was asked to name the greatest fast bowler of his generation it was accepted that he would nominate his friend and colleague Lindwall. However, Keith had no hesitation in selecting Fred.

Keith said: "Statistics prove that Fred was the best. He could swing the ball and not every fast bowler can do this. His action was a delight to watch and his will to win never faltered. Fred was the greatest."

CRICKET IN THE DALES

Fred had a great affiliation with Dales cricket. He played it until he was 57 and Pateley Bridge, Appletreewick, Sedbergh, Cracoe and Settle were grounds where he turned the clock back, changed into whites and proved to the local population that he could still "bowl a decent over or two".

One of his favourite fixtures was an annual friendly. A Yorkshire team of 'oldies' played at Middleham against stable boys, jockeys and trainers with the intention of raising money for charities – not least the local youth club. This catered for boys and girls employed in the stables based at the village often described as 'the Newmarket of the North',

Mrs Lennie Peacock, wife of the late trainer Richard, invariably organised the Middleham opposition. Her husband was the son of Matt Peacock, who trained Dante, the last Yorkshire horse to win the Derby. Lennie's team of cricketers did not exactly measure up in class when compared with the Trueman team so the rules were often altered to make the game more competitive.

It was decided in one encounter that Brian Close would bowl right-handed which he did. He took all ten wickets so he put them in again and this time bowled them out with his left-arm deliveries.

Another highlight of that particular match was the sight of Tony Nicholson fielding on the boundary. It was different in as much as he was mounted on a thoroughbred. Before Tony returned to his native Yorkshire to join the county side he was abroad working as a mounted military policemen in Rhodesia.

Fred said: "The boundary was the best place for Tony. He was a lovely lad and a great bowler. But he was no fielder. We had magnificent fielders in the Yorkshire side with Phil Sharpe the daddy of them all. I was also a bit nifty close to the batsman, but the bravest was Closey. I've seen him stop full-blooded drives with his ankles, legs and other parts of his anatomy. He never flinched. He was a one-off."

Fred claimed that the signs of the impending arrival of spring were easy to detect. He said: "You would see the buds on trees and in the hedgerow. You would listen to the birds chirping and also hear the cricket ball thundering into Brian Close's body."

Fred's presence in the Dales was welcomed by the majority of residents. He believed his cricket prowess helped in that direction and he found the majority of those fortunate to be born in 'God's own county' hospitable and kind. He once commented: "The locals are not rude and they are friendly. People shout 'Hello Fred - how are you doing?' And they don't keep bashing my head about cricket!"

Cricketing Moments

Fred said of youngsters: "We had a ground at my home village of Stainton, near Bawtry, and it hurts me when youths complain that they lack facilities for one game or another. We had to build our own cricket ground when I was a kid and the reward came when we were able to play the sport we loved. We had home-made cricket bats. We lacked the proper tackle. But we enjoyed life and did not have the money or the help children have today. The children should make the most of their good fortune and if they enjoy cricket dedicate themselves to one day playing for our great county. They can't all succeed but making the effort is a worthwhile exercise."

Fred as a youngster with unruly hair, dirty face, and a smile that suggests mischief.

***

Polly Umrigar was Fred Trueman's 'bunny'. The prolific scorer with 3,631 Test runs to his credit was never happy when facing the fiery Yorkshireman. It was 1952 when he arrived in England with the Indian side and he faced Fred who was at the peak of his career.

Polly admitted that he "ran away from the stumps waving his bat in front of him". He was scared and entitled to be wary of the man who packed aggression in his searing pace. Fred dismissed him four times in the four match series hitting the wickets three times.

The Indian was regarded as a master batsman and a 'run machine' but he finished the Tests with an average of 6.14 and a total of 43 runs. Polly did play recognised bowlers like Wes Hall and Roy Gilchrist with style and aplomb. But he simply went to pieces when he faced Fred.

When Polly was up against Trueman at Old Trafford he walked to the crease and hollered: "Your bowling is not bad today Fred."

Fred replied: "It's not meant to be Polly." Then he bowled him.

Polly was 80 when he died four months after Fred's passing.

***

April 20, 1998, was a special day for Fred, who learned that he had become the first player to be installed into the Professional Cricketers' Association Hall of Fame. He was the first bowler to take 300 Test wickets and was honoured at a fund-raising dinner in the Long Room at Lord's.

Fred said: "To be included in the Hall of Fame at all is a great honour. But to be inaugurated as number one is overwhelming. I never expected this."

The PCA will choose 120 of the world's finest cricketers to go into the Hall of Fame in forthcoming years. They will be selected by fans, commentators and players.

Fred made a speech in which he pleaded for cricket to be returned to schools' sporting curriculum, adding: "It is important we attract youngsters to the game and show them that the structure is there to offer them good careers as players."

He was also scornful of a suggestion that international players needed sessions with professional motivators to get the best out of them when they play for England.

Fred said: "Wearing the three lions on our shirt should be motivation enough. If that doesn't motivate players then nothing will."

***

When Fred signalled his retirement with no going back John Arlott penned: "For the sake of such a mighty reputation he is wise to go now. But English cricket will be the poorer, in ability and character, for his going. It is improbable that the game will ever again know quite such another."

***

"Neither of us were worried who got the wickets as long as we were in our favourite positions, our feet up, watching England play." Said by Brian Statham and Fred who together often opened the attack for England.

Fred always called Brian 'George' or 'Kangaroo' because of his long, lean, build.

***

Stories galore - on and off the field - are attributed to Fred. Many are figments of imagination and others carry some semblance of truth. One cast iron tale concerns the Australian player Norman O'Neill, who was sat next to Fred when they waited in the departure lounge at Bombay Airport.

Norman pointed at a couple of Indian gentlemen and murmured: "I think those two Indians are talking about you Fred."

Fred replied: "You're probably right Norman. Folk are talking about me all over the world."

***

If you are concerned about Yorkshire County Cricket Club's lack of success in recent years take heart from Fred's prediction made to his great pal Michael Parkinson.

Fred forecast: "One day Yorkshire will rise like a Spartacus from the ashes."

***

When a Dales cricketer was dismissed he complained: "I didn't touch the ball. I wasn't out."

The umpire replied: "Read tomorrow's paper."

***

When talks were taking place to allow 'foreigners' to play for Yorkshire, Fred threatened to tear up his membership card. Fred was an honorary life member and he declared: "Only those born in the White Rose county should be eligible for the Yorkshire side."

Fred accused four committee men of "making the worst of a bad job".

***

"Fast bowlers are a breed apart and Fred Trueman was apart from the breed," said Denis Compton of England and Middlesex fame.

Part 3

Off the Pitch

Fred Trueman away from the cricket field

LOVE OF THE DALES

Fred has always held strong opinions on his Yorkshire birthright. He was born about three hundred yards from the Nottinghamshire border and might easily have bowled at Trent Bridge as opposed to fulfilling his Yorkshire birthright and playing for the county when only Yorkshire-born youths had this undoubted privilege.

He claimed: "Ninety-nine per cent of people in sport round the world do not like Yorkshire people. It is a toss up between Australians and Yorkshire folk who are disliked more. I found that out as I moved about the world. Yorkshire is unique in as much as we can't get on with each other. For instance, South Yorkshire people are opposed to those born in the North and West Yorkshire people have their foibles. Is there any wonder that Yorkshire County Cricket Club had problems with folk from different parts of the county pulling in different directions?

"That is probably why I decided to settle in the Dales. I believe I passed muster and was accepted after a trial run. Folk are easy-going. We knew places where we could get a pint at midnight and I remember meeting chaps three or four days after the Pateley Bridge show and asking if they enjoyed the day only to be told that they were still on their way home. People here know how to enjoy themselves.

"Eventually I played at Cracoe and invited a lot of famous professional players to turn out there. It took me back again to my childhood when we had sheep running about between overs. Cracoe is not a bad little pitch -– not quite level but better than it used to be."

Fred's love of the Dales never wavered. He always marvelled at the vast acreage of the part of Yorkshire he loved with all the ardour and passion of one fortunate to be born in a place he believed was fashioned in heaven. The Dales will not be the same without its adopted son, celebrated resident and number one fan.

FROM THE TRUEMAN FAMILY ALBUM

Opposite: The Trueman family members were closely knit with Arthur (left) and Fred brothers-in-arms. Arthur also played cricket to a high standard but, much against his father Alan's will, he opted for employment in the local pit.

Arthur and Alan were regulars at matches in which Fred was playing and they were present when he 'ran riot' for England against India at Old Trafford. When Fred bowled Polly Umrigar the ball shattered the wickets and one piece of bail flew just a yard or two short of the boundary. Fred later collected it and gave it to Arthur who had it mounted in a showcase. Presumably the prized souvenir is still in the Trueman family.

When Fred was invited to perform the opening ceremony at the Cricketers Arms, Sheffield, he was accompanied by his mother Ethel. She was a devoted mum to her family of seven children with Fred the middle one. He always claimed his "speed, rhythmic approach and good follow through" resulted in him making a surprise entry into the world. He was delivered by his grandmother within minutes of his mum realising her time was due. He weighed 14lb 10oz.

Ethel appears to be holding a Babycham glass. It was once a very popular drink for ladies.

Fred was never reluctant to fly the flag for his beloved Yorkshire. He counted it a privilege to be born in the Broad Acres and was a fine ambassador for the county.

He was invited to launch the new Tourist Board logo at Rudding Park and thoroughly enjoyed the experience. "They couldn't have picked a better man" was his modest reaction to the invitation.

There was a time when you could pick up an Ashley Jackson original painting for £40 but today you would have to add another couple of noughts to the price. Ashley is not only a superb artist producing Yorkshire Dales scenes of outstanding beauty, but he is also - like Fred - blessed with a charitable heart and it is impossible to estimate how much money the pair has helped to raise for worthy causes.
The bat in the picture was probably an auction prize for one charity or another.
Ashley has many friends in the Yorkshire cricket ranks and indeed the English camp. He and Fred were great buddies and mutual admirers of their respective talents.

Fred was entitled to be proud to receive an OBE but conceded that he felt very humble when he was summoned to Buckingham Palace for the conferring ceremony. There was a feeling in many quarters that a higher honour for his services to cricket would not have been out of place. But Fred was both delighted and surprised when news arrived of his prestigious OBE.

He said: "I have always been loyal to Her Majesty and our country. She is gracious, affable and we had quite a conversation when she pinned on my medal. Although our chat lasted only a minute or two, I feel she recognised my face. It was a day I would never forget."

Fred cut a handsome figure in his morning attire – topper and tails – and he shared the palace limelight with his wife Veronica.

Fred met royalty on many occasions. He was a guest at the British Achievers Luncheon when once again he was able to converse with the Queen. He said: "I believe my OBE was recognition of my services to charity as opposed to cricket."

But it was possibly a reward for both activities and richly deserved.

(Left and over the page) Photographs from the famous red book presented to Fred when he appeared on 'This is Your Life' in October 1979.

(Page 84, left to right, top to bottom) Eamonn Andrews springs the surprise on Fred; daughter Rebecca and son Rodney; Anne and Peter Varley – from RAF days; former team mates Tom Graveney and Ken Barrington; Neil Hawke – Fred's 300th victim; Brian Close.

(Page 85, left to right, top to bottom) Bill Alderson; group including Johnny Wardle, Tony Nicholson, Don Brennan, Mike Smith, John Edrich and Jim Laker; Marylebone Calypso Club is reborn; sharing a joke with Leslie Crowther; Fred's late father Alan features in a rare piece of documentary film; Fred with the red book, flanked by son Rodney, wife Veronica and mother Ethel.

Katherine Worsley was a regular spectator at Headingley matches when her father Sir William Worsley was president of the Yorkshire County Cricket Club. When she married and became the Duchess of Kent her visits were fewer but she never relinquished her support for the Yorkshire side. In this picture the Duchess greeted Fred and his wife Veronica at Headingley – the scene of the fast bowler's many triumphs.

When Fred decided to hang up his boots Sir Williams pleaded with him to reconsider retirement. Sir William said: "Don't do it Fred. You can go on forever. You are still one of the best bowlers in the world."

But Fred would not change his mind and he was later asked if he would choose a farewell gift. He selected a Charles II silver cruet at a cost of £220. He had to pay half because of a 100 guineas limit imposed by the committee. When he arrived home with the cruet he discovered that it was not inscribed. There was no official presentation – just the handing over of a cardboard box containing the retirement present.

Opposite: Fred captured in pensive mood in front of the painting reproduced on page 4. The work of art hangs in the picturesque Trueman home near Gargrave. He always wore his blazer with 'genuine pride'.

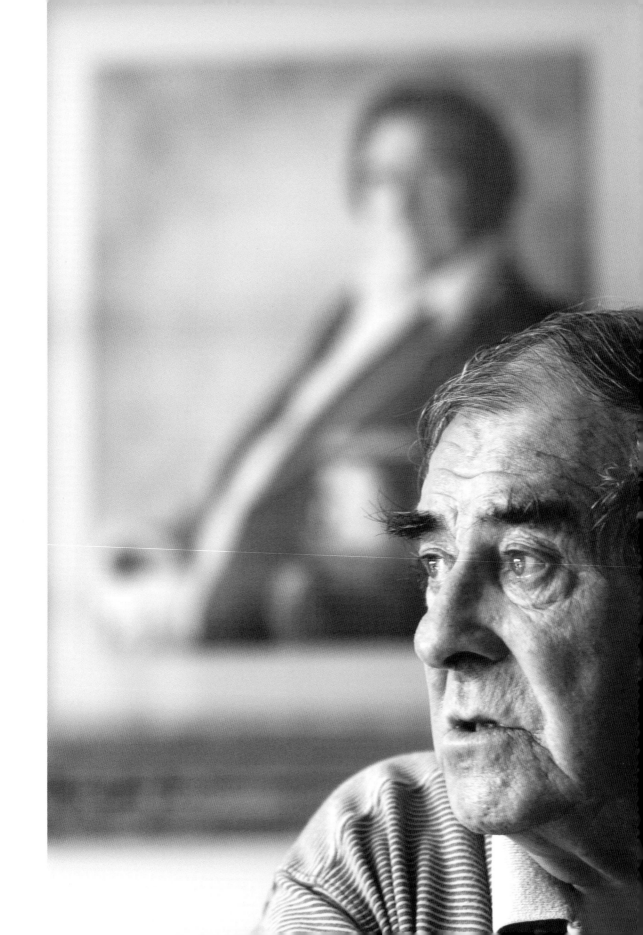

It was June 1991 when the paparazzi and a veritable circus of media representatives invaded the peace, tranquillity and picturesque normality of the Yorkshire Dales. The occasion was a ceremony to bless the marriage of Fred's daughter Rebecca to Damon Welch, an aspiring actor, fitness trainer and son of a Hollywood superstar.

Damon's mother, Raquel Welch, was described by Fred as "a little smasher" and he added: "She is not only lovely – she's a human being."

The world-famous film star returned the compliment with her view of Fred as a "truly lovely, lovely, man".

Raquel was also generous in praise of the Dales, saying: "I've fallen in love with this part of the world. It is beautiful. I have never seen anything like it. I can only describe it as a poem, a beautiful poem."

Raquel entranced staff at the Devonshire Arms, Bolton Abbey, She was radiant and her revealing dress for the church service was described by a lady as "one to die over".

The Dales continues to charm visitors with its unspoiled territory, with views and hues that change with the onset of differing seasons. But sadly the fairytale marriage ended abruptly fifteen months after the blessing in the historic Priory at Bolton Abbey. Rebecca was heartbroken when she rang Fred from America with the news and admitted that the marriage "was not working".

Fred said: "Rebecca was obviously distraught. She explained that it was an amicable break-up with nobody else involved. It's tragic because I thought they were a wonderful couple and so in love. But these things happen."

Later he confided: "The marriage didn't last as long as my run-up. It is very sad and no doubt Rebecca and Damon will recover from the unhappy situation."

Our photographs show:

– Raquel Welch and Fred at the entrance to the centuries-old Priory at Bolton Abbey, where a few years later family and friends gathered for the legendary cricketer's funeral service.

– Fred and his beautiful daughter Rebecca, who has a twin brother Rodney.

Two faces of Fred, both painted by the noted portrait artist John Blakey in 2005. Fred much appreciated the caricature.

Fred celebrated his biblical allocation of three-score-years-and-ten with a drink and presentation at the Sawley Arms, near Ripon. "Seventy not out!" hollered Fred when he was greeted by landlady June Hawes, who provided the appropriate present – a bottle of the 'hard stuff'.

Fred's loyalty to one of his favourite pubs was reflected in an invitation to perform the opening ceremony of the cottages adjoining the Sawley Arms. Fred had the job taped and provided the cutting edge at the request of June Hawes.

Previous page: It took many years for Fred's garden at his home near Gargrave to achieve horticultural perfection. Fred is pictured near his rockery and he often spent hours surveying the picturesque surroundings and studying the various birds paying their regular visits to the Trueman homestead. Fred's father Alan was a keen gardener and obviously imbued his offspring with an appreciation of all things rural.

Fred said: "My love for the Dales intensified after my initial visit. I was determined to live in this beautiful region. When Veronica and me were courting we spotted a stone-built bungalow with extensive land. I put down a deposit and Veronica and I had a home of our own."

Countless hours of work on the building and garden came to fruition with the magnificent home the envy of many.

Today, the home near Gargrave is picturesque and a memorial to a love affair which blossomed after both Fred and Veronica had emerged from broken marriages. It developed into a deep and meaningful relationship leading to marriage which lasted over thirty years.

Fred described Veronica as "the best thing that had ever happened to me and it began on the first day we met." Veronica was the one who inspired his successful career on the after-dinner circuit, keeping the diary, dealing with agents and supporting and guiding him through business and social commitments. Fred called her his "bedrock and the love of his life."

Veronica nursed him through one serious illness. He recovered and they shared an idyllic relationship for years before Fred's final setback. He bore it with typical courage and humour even though he was aware of the inevitable outcome. In the last sentence of his book 'As It Was' he wrote of his enduring love for Veronica – sentiments he also expressed in recorded tapes he left for posterity.

PEACE AND SHEER BEAUTY

There was a time when Fred regularly accepted invitations to join shooting parties on the Yorkshire grouse moors. But interest in bagging birds gave way to friendly conservation and he explained that he preferred to observe the one-time quarries in their natural habitat as opposed to "blowing them out of the sky".

Fred's home and beautiful gardens nestle away from prying eyes near Gargrave. He extended the single storey building he bought in 1970 and the manicured gardens became a home for birds and other wildlife.

Fred never tired of extolling the varied attractions of his picturesque homestead and the regular visits of the winged friends to his impressive property. He spoke with obvious affection and admiration for the 136 species of birds that apparently flutter to the Trueman abode on a daily basis. One might ask how Fred could be so dogmatic about the different examples of birdlife but one rarely questioned his statements and it was prudent to accept the figure 136.

"They seem to know they are on safe ground," said Fred, who listed among his feathered friends: pheasants, robins, wrens, woodpeckers, finches and a cock robin which had the temerity to tap on a window to remind Fred to fill the bird table with breakfast.

Nearly four decades have elapsed since Fred began his love affair with the Yorkshire Dales. The move from town life to the countryside he termed as "one of the best decisions of my life" and he added: "I was completely captivated by the peace, tranquillity and sheer beauty."

It was cricket that first brought him to the countryside and he blessed the day he joined a Yorkshire cricket team in a pre-season warm up game at Settle. He often recalled: "It was the general calm that impressed me most and, although I did not know anything about life in the Dales or even how far this beautiful part of Yorkshire stretched, I was determined to become part of it. It was a step into the unknown I never regretted."

Fred's first sortie took him to Grassington, Kettlewell and on to Aysgarth where he discovered the famous waterfalls, before continuing to the Buttertubs beloved of tourists. He believed there was no end with a fresh vista greeting him round every bend. It was sparsely populated and he stood in silent appraisal of the panoramic scene.

Fred said: "I was brought up in the countryside and knew that this was the place for me. It was like a dream. At the time I was living in Scarborough so this was a complete change of environment.

"Eventually I found this place with my wife Veronica and with a lot of hard work made it what it is today. Of course, there was a lot to do but the effort was justified. Eventually it became the most idyllic place to live. I love it. We are just two miles from the nearest village but close enough to catch a train to London via Leeds.

"We worried about being snowed in during the winter period but this only happened on about four occasions and because we are at the heart of the agricultural area, surrounded by farms, the authorities tend to keep the roads open if only to allow the milk vehicles a clear passage."

Fred believed he was quickly accepted by the majority of people who traced their Dales ancestry back centuries but was always aware that he would be regarded as an 'offcumden'. But Fred's worries on that score were eased when his good friend David Joy revealed that his family has a three hundred year association with the Dales but is still occasionally eyed by other residents with 'an air of suspicion' and regarded as 'not really local!'

'THE GREATEST LIVING YORKSHIREMAN'

The late Baron Wilson of Rievaulx was a mere Right Honourable politician when he made an indelible mark on the respective lives of cricket legend Frederick Sewards Trueman and virtually unknown sports journalist John Morgan. The scene was a private reception room at the Queens Hotel, Leeds, where selected guests gathered before being summoned to enjoy the Variety Club's annual sportsmen's dinner.

Fred and me were invited to address the political leader as 'Harold', who was in talkative mood and reflected on his deep affection for sport and his passionate love for Huddersfield Town football club. Harold recalled that he had recently attended a match at Craven Cottage, London, where Fulham were at home to his beloved Leeds Road team.

Harold said: "The guest next to me in the directors' box was the Bishop of Fulham and his support for the Cottagers was obviously as strong as mine for Huddersfield. The game was in its infancy when the Fulham left-winger broke clear and raced down the touchline. He hit a high cross to the Huddersfield goal area where the inside left missed his attempted header by inches. The centre-forward completely miskicked and the inside right failed to connect as the right winger charged into to crash the ball over the bar with the Town goalie stranded."

Harold added: "At this point the Bishop was frantic. He trembled with excitement and at each miss he murmured: 'Oh f…f…f….' And I said to myself: 'Harold you are about to hear for the first time an ecclesiastical obscenity.' But the near-demented clergyman simply shook his head and murmured in pious tones: 'Oh folly, folly, folly!'"

Fred and me exchanged glances and fell about with laughter during the ensuing dinner. It was a great success and the occasion when pipe-smoking Harold paid an oft-quoted tribute to Fred who was also a devotee of the noxious weed. Harold described Fred as 'the greatest living Yorkshireman' and the bashful sportsman's demure reaction was: "Who am I to contradict such a powerful political force?"

It was a title Harold repeated on other occasions in spite of Fred's loyal allegiance to the Conservative party and the opposition to the Huddersfield man destined to become Labour's Prime Minister.

Harold had met Fred for the first time when they were invited to a book launch at a Foyle's Literary Luncheon. Harold said: "Meeting Fred was like greeting my own Walter Mitty in real life. I can see him now extirpating the infidel, whether it be Lancashire at Old Trafford or Australia at Headingley. Luckily he has never had, as I have, a catch dropped at square leg in the Soviet Union by a member of the secret police!"

Fred produced his pipe and tobacco pouch and invited Harold to fill his pipe. Fred later said: "He did it with the panache of a Yorkshireman. There are six million Yorkshire males and he has described me as the greatest. I can think of only one man who would agree with Harold. That is me."

Harold Wilson described Fred as "Yorkshire's greatest living Yorkshireman", despite the fact that the international sportsman did not subscribe to the Huddersfield-born Prime Minister's political persuasion.

Fred was a Margaret Thatcher supporter, an avowed Conservative, and also a pacifist. Although his idol was Winston Churchill, he once said: "I am totally against wars. Arguments can be settled without recourse to weapons. Mind you I would always be ready to serve my Queen and country. I think our Queen is a wonderful lady and a fine ambassador and example to us all."

Another Prime Minister much better known to Fred was John Major. When politics demanded his presence, his passion for watching cricket at various grounds was curtailed. But, when the chance to indulge in his favourite recreation came, he took full advantage. He even managed occasional visits to Headingley, especially when Test matches were ongoing.

John and Fred were reciprocal in their admiration of each other's talent and occupation. John would dearly have loved life as a professional cricketer but it is a safe bet that Fred would not have deserted the sport for life in the House of Commons.

Fred in political circles again, confiding his views to Baroness Shirley Vivien Teresa Brittain Williams. She was awarded a Life Peerage in 1993.

Fred's friend was simply Shirley Williams when she became a Labour MP in 1964. She held many ministerial posts before becoming a co-founder of the Social Democratic Party and later a member of the Social and Liberal Democratic Party.

THE PHIL JOHN AWARD

A few years later Fred was invited to attend another Variety Club's Player of the Year Dinner as a guest of the Rothmans tobacco company. The table was organised by Brian Clark, Chairman of Infopress, who handled Rothmans publicity. It was Brian who asked Fred to act for the company with bids at the inevitable charity auction of sporting items.

Fred's budget was in the region of £500. But he had the bit between his teeth and he was still bidding when competition for a special silver salver had reached three times the stipulated amount. The unique item was knocked down to Fred. It was a salver made to commemorate the Centenary Cup Final played at Wembley where Leeds United beat Arsenal by one goal. It carries the engraved signatures of all the players who took part in that memorable fixture. But Rothmans and Brian Clark did not know what to do with the item or how best to capitalise on Fred's unexpected generosity on behalf of the reluctant owners of the bauble.

At that time I was writing for the Yorkshire Evening Post's sports pages under the pseudonym 'Phil John'. The name was coined out of the editor Malcolm Barker's plea to me that he had "two columns to fill John". The centenary salver was given to me to use as 'The Phil John Award for services to Amateur Sport'. Winners of the trophy held it for a month and were given a replica on its return. Competition for the award was extremely keen and Rothmans certainly gained plenty of publicity in the days before tobacco advertising was banned.

Fred was all in favour of the scheme, which acknowledged the contribution made to sport by those who toiled in the background with scant reward for their noble activities. In fact, Fred made a couple of the presentations at the celebrations that usually accompanied the award ceremonies.

The salver was won by men and women from all walks of life and well cared for until the occasion when it was returned in a dreadful condition. The winner – a retired miner – had obviously used it as a dinner plate. His knife and fork had gouged crevices and scratches in the surface and obliterated some of the signatures.

Fred and me saw the funny side of the winner's treatment of his prize but Rothmans' PR advisers and the Yorkshire Evening Post hierarchy were not amused. Leeds jewellers Greenwoods did a fine repair job on the salver and another was made at great expense in case of a similar incident. Both are now on display in the National Football Museum where they are behind glass and nestle on blue velvet with viewers oblivious of the history of this prized trophy.

You can imagine Fred's reaction when he was asked to contribute to the salver's restoration and replacement.

"I would rather not," smiled Fred.

THE PROFESSIONAL LOSERS' CLUB

Fred Trueman was the recipient of countless awards, including a prized OBE, but there was one title he politely declined – presidency of the Professional Losers' Club.

The invitation to accept the doubtful honour was extended by me following a sortie to the Tyne Tees Television area.

Lawrie Higgins, who was Head of Sport at Yorkshire TV, and John Meade, who introduced Britain's television audience to Countdown, accompanied Fred to the North East to publicise Indoor League. This was a YTV production presented by Fred and it eventually was networked on ITV with Fred on view nationwide and signing off with "I'll sithee!"

The return journey from Newcastle was broken with a visit to the Forrester's Arms, Kilburn, to take on food and alcohol. This popular pub nestles beneath the rolling Hambleton Hills and is adjacent to the famous furniture factory established by Robert "Mousey" Thompson. When Fred, Lawrie, John and me arrived at the hostelry the late John Mayne was mine host and one of his regular customers was Bob Cartwright who married into the Thompson family. Bob was boss of the internationally known firm.

John Mayne accepted the fact that he was widely regarded as the rudest landlord in Yorkshire. People flocked to put the claim to the test and John rarely disappointed the visitors. But in real life he was a charming, charitable and friendly character and, of course, belligerent and bad-tempered when the occasion demanded.

John was not only a publican – an occupation which probably contradicted his background. He was educated at Ampleforth, and born into a hugely wealthy bookmaking business. He was also related to the Leeds family of Pickersgills, owners of a leading printing firm.

John was on reluctant bar duty when we entered the premises and he had no idea of the fame or standing of one of cricket's most famous sons, or the television background of the others. Not that he would have been impressed or more the wiser.

Conversation turned to racing with the arrival of Jack Calvert, who trained a team of horses at historic stables at the summit of Sutton Bank, and it was then Fred was invited to membership of the turf brotherhood founded by a group of unlucky punters. They made the Forresters Arms their headquarters and the rules of the club were:

> *Grin when you win.*
> *Laugh when you lose.*
> *Win or lose*
> *We'll have some booze.*

If a member boasted about his winnings he was fined a bottle of champagne. If one moaned about losses he paid the same penalty. It was a no-win situation with champagne corks flying in all directions when the members returned to the pub from an unsuccessful sortie to the local Thirsk racecourse.

Fred wisely rejected the invitation to join the committee on three counts.

> *– He was not that keen on champagne.*
> *– He wasn't often in the vicinity.*
> *– He never envisaged being a 'loser' at anything.*

He was hell-bent on emerging as a winner and this was an obvious trait in his approach to cricket at the lowest and highest levels. He was not only a winner at sport but life in general.

Fred later told us that he started playing cricket at school when he was five years old and he had to win. His sister Flo chastised him for bowling as fast at girls as he did at boys. But he argued that he was a winner.

He said: "Even when we played tiddlywinks I had to emerge as the best. And there was no way I wanted to lose at cricket. I remember bowling and batting for hours on end in a yard adjoining an orchard owned by Farmer Middleton. We nicked a few plums and apples in between bowling at a wicket made from a dustbin lid standing on two bricks.

"I also remember when I saw my first major cricket ground. It was the one at Sheffield and it took my breath away. The only fields I had seen as big as that cricket pitch had turnips or wheat in them."

We enjoyed our short halt at the Forrester Arms and my favourite story of this pub concerns the day a party of Americans called to put the rudest landlord claim to the test. John Mayne did not let them down and one of the visitors pointed to the huge oak tree towering in the ground at the entrance to the pub. He asked if there was any historical significance in this impressive tree.

"Yes," replied John, "When the famous highwayman Dick Turpin broke out of his London prison he rode his mare Black Bess to York. He was followed by the Bow Street Runners who almost captured him. But Dick Turpin escaped by hiding in that very same oak tree."

The American was suitably impressed and he repeated the story to his tourists before they took their leave still discussing the saga of that infamous highwayman.

Twelve months later another collection of Americans arrived at the Forresters. John was there to greet them and the ladies and gentlemen made the trip to Yorkshire specifically to gaze at the famous 'Tip Durkin Tree'.

It remained a memorial to 'Tip Durkin' until John died and the legend went with him to the grave. Sadly, so did the Professional Losers' Club.

None laughed louder or longer than Fred Trueman when he heard the tale of 'Tip Durkin' – another chapter in Yorkshire's folklore.

ACTS OF KINDNESS

Fred was not a paragon of virtue. We are told that a just man falls seven times a day and Fred often exceeded the biblical quota. However, in his allotted attributes was loyalty. He maintained this with countless friends he made in and out of the sport he cherished.

Fred's affinity with Birmingham businessman Alan Carter goes back decades and was fostered after a slight 'tiff'. Alan recalls: "I was at a charity dinner where Fred conducted an auction to raise money for a worthy cause. One of the items was a cricket bat and the bidding rose by fivers to forty pounds with only me and another chap involved.

"Fred decided to hurry things along and announced: 'The first chap to bid £50 will get the bat.' And a man, not involved in the early exchanges, shouted 'fifty' and collected the bat.

"It was annoying because I really wanted it and made my feelings known to Fred after the dinner ended. His response was: 'Don't get excited – I have another three autographed bats in the car. You can have one for nowt.'

"Fred duly handed over the bat and, in passing, mentioned that he was representing a Sheffield oil firm. I owned a factory with a huge oil consumption and I asked him to ring me the following day. I had never met Fred before the dinner and I was delighted when he made contact. I gave him his first order for oil – somewhere in the region of £20,000 and our relationship started and continued from that day to his funeral."

Alan's memories could fill a book. Whenever Fred attended Edgbaston Tests or county matches he stayed with Alan and his wife Susie. They enjoyed many a lengthy wine-fuelled conversation with Alan admiring Fred's prodigious memory for cricket facts, hilarious stories and an enviable resistance to alcohol.

Alan recalled: "Fred loved a bottle of wine or two, and sometimes three, almost as much as me. He also enjoyed talking about wildlife – particularly birds. His knowledge was impressive even to me and my wife. We are both experts on the subject. However, I once impressed Fred when I told him that I often hand-fed foxes. Although we lived in Birmingham and well away from fields we had visiting foxes which came round most evenings. When I gained their trust they often allowed me to feed them. Fred was lost in admiration. The only time I bettered Fred."

Alan remembers so many of Fred's acts of kindness and particularly one related to a dinner party held by students on the intersection of a stretch of Birmingham's notorious motorway. Alan picked Fred up from the Edgbaston ground where he had been taking part in Test Match Special. They were heading for a Chinese restaurant where diners had to take their own wine and they were calling at an off-licence shop to buy the bottles.

Alan recalled: "Fred wondered if the students had remembered the port to go with their dinner. We parked the car and walked over to the partygoers on the central reservation of the very busy road. We were told that the students were studying medicine and – with the exception of one – they were celebrating passing their exams.

"Fred was immediately recognised. We provided the port and it was nine o'clock before we took our leave. However, Fred had discovered the identity of the one student who had failed his exam. He was a bit miffed and Fred promised him that if he was successful when he resat the exams in November we would return and celebrate the feat in style on the very same spot.

"The young 'medic' passed and Fred kept his promise. We all turned up in dinner jackets and black ties and we had a memorable dinner, with port. One of the Sunday papers had wind of the party and covered the festivities. Perhaps Fred tipped them off? Fred certainly pushed the boat out and the students enjoyed every moment and every drop."

Alan also treasures the memory of Fred inviting him to join a host of celebrities on the top table in a tribute dinner to the late Brian Statham. He said: "Fred surveyed the scene packed with famous folk. He sipped his wine and said: 'Not bad for a miner's son.'

"Fred never forgot his roots or his humble but happy background and he was entitled to be proud of his achievements and contribution to cricket and life in general."

THE SPORT OF KINGS

Ted Gifford was a successful racehorse trainer based in Skipton and he was just as adept at producing winners on the Flat as he was preparing jumpers for the hurly-burly of the National Hunt scene. It was Ted who persuaded local solicitor Jack Mewies and his great friend Fred to own a racehorse in partnership.

Fred was no stranger to the equine world. His father Alan was attached to Earl Fitzwilliam's stables at Wentworth Woodhouse where he served an apprenticeship and blossomed into a top-class rider. Fred was proud of the fact that his dad rode winners under National Hunt rules and also in the point-to-point sphere. Weight problems and injuries cut short Alan's riding career and he reluctantly left the employment of local racehorse owner Captain Adcock to take a job as a miner.

Fred's grandfather Albert Trueman was also involved with horses on the buying and selling front so the boy destined to become a cricket legend was no stranger to man's four-legged friends.

Fred's friendship with Jack Mewies began when they met at Scarborough Cricket Festival in the 1950s. It was an association destined to last decades and they also became business partners and joint owners of the company Fred Trueman Sports Ltd.

Their entry into ownership of a racehorse was blessed with moderate success. Their first horse, St Maur, ran a promising race at Thirsk and showed good speed before tiring and finishing out of the first three. Fred was present to watch the horse in action but possibly earned more by taking part in a television sports programme broadcast from the Yorkshire track.

Fred gave tips to racegoers who surrounded him but his fancies were wide of the mark. "Stick to cricket Fred," said one punter and his pals nodded agreement.

Their second horse 'Lynton Croft' recorded two victories before Fred and Jack Mewies moved into ownership and the filly was ridden to victory by an apprentice called Harold Wilson. Fred said: "This is probably an omen. Harold will probably ride her again even though I don't subscribe to Mr Harold Wilson's political beliefs."

Jack was a keen racegoer and, although Fred expressed great interest in the Sport of Kings, he gave me the opinion that cricket, rugby and football were more to his sporting appetite. Racehorse ownership can also be an expensive financial pastime and I remember Fred telling me that his dad regularly advised him "never to buy owt that eats owt".

Fred was not a gambler. He said: "The only time I backed a horse it was into the shafts."

I enjoyed a couple of days with Fred at Doncaster races and also recall, with a tinge of nostalgia, his contribution to the annual St Leger Dinner which was held for close on two hundred years on the eve of the big race. Sadly, the function was abandoned ten years ago and Fred was among the last batch of after-dinner speakers to grace the Mansion House celebration of the world's oldest Classic.

Fred was in brilliant form and it was quite an honour for a man not employed in the racing game to be given the task of making the principal speech at this celebrated function. Many of the Press reporters and television types were booked in the nearby Danum Hotel and joined Fred at the bar for an hour or two to continue his story telling.

In recent years Fred attended meetings at York racecourse and it was there at a non-racing function he was given a surprise presentation. It was an award for his lifelong contribution to cricket, sport, the media and his beloved county.

BED BUT NO BREAKFAST

The wine and beer flowed and was supped with careless abandon at Wharfedale Rugby Union Club's annual dinner where I was on 'talking duty' at the request of British Lion, England, Yorkshire and one-time Leeds star John Spencer. There was no chance of me driving back to Leeds and Fred Trueman said: "If you get stuck there is a bed at my place."

The offer should have been grabbed with open arms but the late Arthur Chaney, mine host at Grassington's Forester's Arms, interceded with the invitation: "You are stopping at my pub lad and when you wake tomorrow morning I will cook you the biggest breakfast you have ever seen. Arkle the steeplechaser would not be able to jump over it. I don't care what time you wake me. Just call and the breakfast will be on the table when you come out of the shower."

Arthur was a regular at northern racecourses. We were good pals and it would not have been gracious to reject his offer of bed and breakfast. We had more drinks in the Forester's. Fred had long departed and when I asked Arthur to direct me to my bed he tossed me a blanket and invited me to sleep on a bench in the taproom.

Before he turned off the light he said: "I don't care what time you wake. Just shake me and I will get to work with the frying pan."

It was 6.30 am when I shook Arthur's shoulder. He opened one eyelid and murmured: "Get lost!"

Those were not his exact words but I got the message. I drove my car to the Yorkshire Evening Post, Leeds, and started work at nine o'clock.

Fred rang me an hour later to ask how I had fared.

"It was wonderful and Arthur was the perfect host," I lied.

Fred knew I was telling 'porkies' but I never admitted the truth to him.

Arthur – like Fred – was a great Yorkshire character. I was at the races when he was taken seriously ill and even today I expect him to turn up at Pontefract or Ripon or Thirsk and ask: "What are we backing today John?"

I will also be looking for Fred at Headingley. Cricket will not be the same without his opinions, grumpy complaints, his rib-tickling jokes and the inevitable comparison of the players in his heyday and the present.

Fred and Cynthia Payne had something in common. They both worked as speakers on the after-dinner circuit. But Cynthia had another string to her bow – a club for gentlemen providing a rather risky and risqué agenda of activities. Cynthia earned the title 'Madam Sin' but she was a welcome visitor to the Trueman homestead.

Part 4

Trueman's Tales

Fred's sense of humour enabled him to make a huge success of his work on the after-dinner circuit and he was also in great demand as a stand-up comedian with a couple of hours' jokes committed to memory.

It was nothing exceptional to have ninety to a hundred speaking engagements in his diary with 'gigs' confirmed as far away as China, Australia, Dubai and Spain, in addition to bookings from Leeds to London. However, he did discover that the Dales humour is so different to that of the quick-fire one-liners employed by city slickers.

Fred realised that the Dales way of life and a brand of comedy was peculiar to this part of Yorkshire and he soon learned that he was not the only 'funny fellow' enjoying a drink and a chat at one of hundreds of well-patronised hostelries.

Fred said: "My old mates Jack Mewies and Dennis Manby were seasoned characters and introduced me to Dales tales. One example came from Dennis who walked out of the Miners Arms at Greenhow and spotted an old farmer he hadn't seen for a week or two.

Dennis asked: 'How are you doing?'

The farmer replied: 'Not so good.'

Dennis persisted: 'You look champion to me. What's wrong?'

His pal murmured: 'I've been fighting drink all my life – and I'll tell you something.'

Dennis asked: "What's that?"

The old fellow shouted: 'I hope the war never finishes!'"

***

Jack Mewies never tired of telling the tale of the Dales man who sought a divorce in the local court.

The judge said: "I'm going to award your wife £5 a week."

The husband replied; "That's very kind of you and I'll try and giver her a bob or two as well."

***

Dennis Manby was never short of a story and he relayed the news that one bloke was thinking of starting up a brothel in the village.

Dennis said: "I told him he would be skint in a week. There are too many at it for nowt round here."

***

This was typical of the Dales sense of fun and so was the tale of the postman who pedalled his bike up a long drive mile after mile to deliver a letter. Eventually he arrived at a farmhouse and the farmer stood on the doorstep to receive his mail.

The postman said: "By God it's a long drive isn't it?"

The farmer replied: "Well if it were any shorter it wouldn't reach!"

***

Fred recalled that his old Yorkshire cricket club captain Ronnie Burnet lived at Pateley Bridge and he talked about the volume of traffic when people flock to the 'Nidderdale Rant', which is the last of the Dales shows towards the end of September.

Fred was no stranger to this part of the Dales. He played cricket at the Pateley showground where many Yorkshire players had turned out in games stretching back nearly a century. They included those cricketing legends Wilfred Rhodes, Herbert Sutcliffe, Len Hutton, George Hurst, Maurice Leyland, Hedley Verity, Johnny Wardle and many others. The game was one of the features of the show and they were given about four pounds each for their overnight stay – a lot of money in those far-off days. The players gave their time because the match was a seasoned tradition and they were honoured to be asked. The match does not take place these days, which is more the pity.

However, Ronnie Burnet was heading for the ground to take part in the match and the traffic was bumper to bumper on the cramped roads leading to the show. It still is quite a feat for cars to pass each other on the narrow lanes and there was one old chap standing at one side and another on the opposite side.

One shouted: "How did you get over there?"

And the other hollered: "I was born on this side."

Fred said: "This was an example of the instant repartee typical of those who were born in this unique part of Yorkshire where folk appear to have more time for a chat than busy residents in the big cities who appear to be short of leisure time."

***

It was the first day of a county match, Yorkshire versus Glamorgan, at Harrogate, when a pensioner paid his entry fee and chatted to the club secretary about the weather and the prospects of an exciting game.

The Harrogate official murmured: "You would have thought there would be more people in the ground on such a lovely day as this."

The elderly supporter remarked: "I wouldn't worry. It'll fill up after lunch."

The secretary asked why that was and the veteran replied: "It's half day closing at Pateley Bridge."

Fred's variety club act with jokes and cricket tales was often preceded by a spectacular entrance. When he made his debut at the Ace of Clubs, Woodhouse, Leeds, he was dressed in full cricket gear with ball in hand. He burst through a paper hoop with a true reflection of his classic bowling action. Of course, he retained his grip on the ball but members of the audience nearest to the stage were not convinced. They all dived for safety.

Later, Fred dropped the cricket clobber but maintained the 'bursting on stage' entrance. He committed scores of jokes to memory and he could ad lib for over two hours without repetition of a gag. Little wonder he was in such great demand as an after-dinner speaker at home and abroad. He was loved from Headingley to Hong Kong and Armley to Australia.

Like many sporting celebrities Fred was a regular entertainer on cruise ships. There was none better than Fred when it came to 'telling the tale' and he topped the bill on this cruise in the West Indies.

Fred liked the story of the chap who went to Scarborough for a weekend and listened to a bloke who walked up and down the promenade shouting: "Seagulls for sale two bob apiece – seagulls for sale two bob apiece."

The holidaymaker handed him two shillings and said: "I'll have one."

The salesman pocketed the cash and pointed to a gull high in the sky.

"That's yours," he said as he walked on shouting "Seagulls for sale."

***

One chap came up from the south of England and booked a room in a pub in Grassington. I think he stayed at the Wilson Arms and he had heard about Yorkshire folk getting up early in the morning to go to work. He decided to put this early rising to the test and he was out of bed at 4am, dressed, and walking through the village.

He met a farmer who was carrying a pail of milk and he nodded: "Good morning, lovely day."

The farmer answered, "Aye, it was first thing."

Fred added: "That is typical of Yorkshire humour in these parts."

***

One of Fred's favourites concerns a couple who visited the Yorkshire Dales for the first time and were greatly impressed by the beauty. The man and his wife met a group of children going to Sunday School and the visitors stopped to have a kindly word with them. They discovered that the kiddies were six brothers and sisters. They were called Brown and lived in a farm just down the road. They couple waved good-bye and walked towards their home where a chap was busy in the garden.

"Would you by any chance be Farmer Brown – father of those lovely children we have been talking to?" asked the man.

"Aye that's right," replied the farmer.

The visitor said: "They're grand kids aren't they? Unfortunately me and my missus haven't any. We've been trying for years without success. But you have six. Could it be anything to do with the Dales air?"

"It could be," said Farmer Brown, "But I've never heard it mentioned before. It might be worth putting it to the test".

The couple then noticed that the farmer did bed and breakfast and the chap said: "If I booked the wife in how long do you think it would take?"

Farmer Brown scratched his head and said: "If I can get the sheep in you could have her back same afternoon."

***

One of the pubs close to Fred's home is The Angel at Hetton, where one of the attractions was the pub dog called Duke. The place would be heaving with customers but it was noticeable that one table with a couple of chairs was always empty. Locals knew the reason why the table and chairs were always deserted but strangers did not and often seized the opportunity to take a seat.

The visitors were not aware that when Duke appeared in the bar he invariably spotted a butterfly or a moth on the premises and he would launch himself at his quarry by using the 'empty' table as a springboard sending pints, glasses, crisps and the lot flying. It was a regular occurrence. The locals loved it but the same could not be said of the customers totally unaware of the dog's antics.

***

The Angel is not far from Cracoe cricket ground where Fred offered his services when he finished his career in first class cricket. He met the secretary of the local village cricket club and the conversation went as follows:

Fred asked: "What league do you play in?"

"The evening league. Twenty-five overs each, and then we go back to the Angel at Hetton for a drink," he replied.

"That sounds like my kind of cricket club."

"Will you be prepared to play for us?"

"Yes – I want to become part of Dales life."

Fred learnt later that the secretary excitedly went back to his committee and announced that Fred Trueman would be very happy to play for them. The meeting went quiet. Then after a long pause it was decreed: "Would you thank Mr Trueman for his very generous offer. But it's batsman we're after – not bowlers!"

Fred adds: "Later I was always made welcome there. I opened the new pavilion. They were given a grant but most of the work was done by the members and players. When I drove past Cracoe I always slowed down to take a look at the cricket field. Nearly every village in Yorkshire had or used to have a ground. It did my old heart good just to know that the game is still played in even the most remote spots in the Dales."

***

Wilfred Pickles, who fronted the popular radio show Have a Go, visited Radio Leeds when the station was housed in the Merrion Centre. He and his wife Mabel joined Fred and me for a drink at the adjoining hotel and we asked Wilfred for his favourite story.

He said: "Bill and Bob were great chums with a real passion for Yorkshire cricket. They were knocking on in years but managed to get to most games and were determined to visit Old Trafford, Manchester, for the annual Roses Match. It was a chilly and damp morning when they boarded the train at Leeds and Bill sat opposite Bob in the compartment as the steam engine slowly pulled out of the old Central station.

Suddenly Bill said: "Bob – your flies are open?"

Bob replied: "Are they?"

Bill confirmed: "They are that."

Bob asked: "What can you see?"

Bill answered: "Everything."

Bob exclaimed: "Everything?"

Bill murmured: "Yes – everything!"

Bob asked: "Is it pink or blue?"

Bill replied: "Blue."

Bob said: "There will be no play at Old Trafford today."

***

One of Fred's favourite yarns concerned the old Yorkshire player and coach George Hirst who before a Roses Match, at Headingley, knelt in an empty dressing room and said a prayer to the Almighty.

He was overheard to plead: "Dear Lord if you want Lancashire to win they will do so. But if you can keep out of this match for the next three days we will knock the living daylight out of them."

***

Fred recalls: "On Sundays about twenty to thirty of us used to meet at the Craven Arms at Appletreewick. Those were the days before the breathalyser. And it is true to say there were not as many cars on the road. Those wonderful days are in the past and consigned to Dales history. Life used to be more casual, relaxed and enjoyable. We had humour too – lots of it. We all had a tale to tell, like another from the Dales concerning a farmer and his wife."

They went to Skipton to do a bit of shopping and the farmer told his missus: "This trip will give me the opportunity to pay some of our spare cash into the bank."

She shopped in the high street and he called in at the local branch of the Abbey. He plonked a tin on the counter and said: "There is ten thousand pounds in there to go into my account."

The cashier counted the notes and said: "Sorry Sir, but I make it nine thousand and ten."

"Count it again," said he. She did and arrived at the same total. Another assistant was asked to count and once again the figure came out at nine thousand and ten.

The Abbey manager was counting the cash when in walked the wife. The farmer told her what had happened and she said: "You daft beggar. You've brought the wrong tin with you."

Little wonder Fred loved the Dales and its humour!

***

Jack and Bessie Barnard were mine hosts at the Craven Arms and often told the tale of lads playing dominoes and drinking pints. It was quite a session and they played and drank. Eventually, one of them said to the landlord: "Would it be possible to put a bit more light on?"

He replied: "Why don't you open the curtains?"

They did and glorious sunshine beamed in on the scene. It was seven in the morning. The lads had played and supped the night away.

Fred said: "There was a lot to be said for the Christian approach many Dales landlords had to the licensing hours and it was quite easy to pop in for one pint and an impromptu party break out."

The marathon domino game occurred when Harry Newbould was landlord. He was quite a character, like so many landlords who dispensed good beer, and were never short of thirsty customers.

***

One of Fred's favourite comics was Albert Modley, who told the tale of a chap leaving a pub in Grassington. The local vicar said: "I'm surprised to see you coming out of a place like that." So the fellow went back in again!

***

Fred recalled another story about a pupil we will call Smith Minor who was educated at Sedbergh Grammar School and was a member of a highly successful cricket team.

Fred said: "Sedbergh had a most wonderful ground. I played there with the MCC and the Forty Club and also our private charity team The Saints. The matches were always very exciting and enjoyable. We even lost to Sedbergh once. It was in the year when the school team were unbeatable and to reward the players for their efforts the Headmaster arranged an educational trip to Paris."

The boys duly arrived and of course saw all the sights – the Eiffel Tower, Notre Dame, Left Bank, the Louvre, the Tomb of Napoleon and enjoyed the hospitality arranged by the French education authority. The Headmaster then came to the conclusion that the boys should attend one of the famous shows and he booked seats for them at the Pigalle. He said: "You will find this very educational because Paris is famous for its night life and wonderful entertainment."

The curtain rose. Sixteen beautiful ladies came on stage dancing and high-kicking. Suddenly they started disrobing much to the discomfort of the Headmaster. The girls peeled off clothes until they were naked as the day they were born with the Headmaster now perspiring and deeply anxious.

Suddenly there was a tap on his back. He turned and said to the boy: "What is it?"

The pupil replied: "It's Smith Minor. His father told him that if he saw anything like this he would turn to stone. He thinks he has already started!"

Fred said: "The story has been told for generations and has become a firm fixture in Dales lore."

***

Jim Swanton, the celebrated cricket journalist and broadcaster, was a rather pompous man. Raymond Illingworth once said: "Jim had a panel in his car so that he didn't have to talk to his chauffeur."

Jim's car broke down in the Dales one Sunday afternoon. He was stranded but a farmer came to his rescue and offered him a lift to a local garage.

Jim said: "I notice you have a panel at the back of your seat. Is this to stop passengers talking to you?"

"No," said the farmer, "It's to stop sheep licking me on the back of my neck when I bring them from market."

***

Fred told the tale of a Yorkshireman who climbed to the top of a mountain to get near enough to talk to God.

Looking up, the Dales man asked: "Lord what does a million years mean to you?"

The Lord replied: "A minute."

The Yorkshire lad persisted: "And what does a million pounds mean to you?"

The Lord replied: "A penny."

The Yorkshireman pleaded: "Can I have a penny?"

The Lord replied: "In a minute!"

***

A Dales pensioner turned to his missus and said: "You will have to forget about the past because we can't change it. We must forget about the future because we can't predict it. Will you also forget about your birthday present because I forgot to buy one?"

***

Fred loved the story of the lady sitting in a railway station waiting room, struggling with her cup of tea, as her train came into view.

The farmer sitting at the next table realised that the lady's tea was very hot and he gallantly offered his. He said: "Take mine lass. I've already blown on it and poured it into t'saucer."

***

This young lad from the Dales took the train to Leeds and called in a Burton's tailoring shop where a salesman approached with the greeting: "And what is your pleasure sir?"

The lad replied: "Rugby, whippets, Tetley's and sometimes sex on a Saturday neet. But for now I'll settle for a blazer and a pair of slacks."

Epilogue

'Goodbye My Friend'

When the news broke on Saturday, July 1, 2006, that Fred Trueman had died, Headingley was the scene of England's one-day international with Sri Lanka. Players on both sides lined-up in a salute to the cricket legend – joined by stunned spectators with many openly grief-stricken at the sombre announcement. The shock news reverberated throughout the cricketing universe. Fred's outstanding achievements at home and on foreign shores were renowned, legendary and immortal.

Headingley was not Fred's favourite ground. He had mixed feelings about Yorkshire's cricket capital. His favourite was the now defunct Bramall Lane where he captained his beloved county to victory over the Australian tourists. However, Headingley was where news of Fred's passing resulted in an impromptu demonstration of love and respect. Young and old joined in a handclapping ripple, which developed into a crescendo before the ground lapsed into a muffled murmur and eventually total silence.

Tributes flowed throughout the days leading to the simple funeral service Fred wanted at the Priory of St Mary and St Cuthbert, Bolton Abbey, and the final resting in a grave, cut on a gentle slope, and adjacent to the church Fred and his widow Veronica knew so well.

The rector, Reverend John Ward, spoke of the "cricket colossus, a man capable of crossing all boundaries and social classes."

Retired umpire Harold 'Dickie' Bird paid tribute with unashamed emotion and tears welled as he echoed the words of many: "Goodbye my friend."

Yorkshire President Bob Appleyard, who once shared the opening Yorkshire attack with Fred, said: "My relationship with him goes back to the 1950s and he enjoyed a remarkable career. Few can compare with his record at County and Test level. Even when he was in the twilight of his cricket life he was still able to take wickets with guile as much as sheer pace."

Former England and Yorkshire captain Brian Close declared: "Fred was a great bowler, a great man, and a great character. His death is a tragedy for Yorkshire cricket. It is a pity that the present generation of cricket followers did not see him play and marvel at his ability. He was a much better bowler than the bowlers are today and he got through a lot more work. He was 100 per cent Yorkshire and England and he never gave up."

Raymond Illingworth, the former England captain, who returned to Yorkshire to lead his native county said: "You hear a lot about how good certain fast bowlers have been. But this fellow was really the best. There is absolutely no doubt about that.

We played for twenty years together from being no more than boys in 1948. And I have lost a great friend and colleague. He was well known for his comments about other players but there was never any malice in what he said. We shall never see his like again."

Fred always described Phil Sharpe as one of the best three slip fielders in the world. Phil rated Fred as "One of the game's greatest fast bowlers. He was a wonderful character in the dressing room and out of it. He will be sadly missed."

Geoffrey Boycott was generous in his praise when he was acquainted with Fred's passing. He said: "Fred was a legend, pure and simple. There are very few people in life you can call by their Christian name and everyone knows exactly who they mean. He was a funny man, an amusing man. He made you laugh and he was a great, great cricketer."

Geoffrey added: "Fred got his Test wickets at 21 runs each and he had the most classical action of all time. It was absolutely perfect. He swung the ball at great pace. He bowled a fantastic yorker, and he had a strong physique that hardly ever broke down. On top of that he was a terrific sportsman. I never heard him swear at an umpire or swear at a batsman. He may have said things at the heat of the moment if a batsman got away with a lucky edge. Who doesn't? But it was never directed at any one individual. Fred always had a way of being funny with it."

We will never again see another Fred Trueman powering in from the Kirkstall Lane end at Headingley or the Pavilion End at Park Avenue, shirt sleeves flapping, that silky acceleration, perfect action, perfect length, and more often than not, the glower which followed as the batsman played and missed or, even worse, managed to make contact and scrape another run to the chagrin of the great man. His vocabulary in such moments was limited but exact.

Trueman was much more than just a fast bowler – how the world "just" would have raised his hackles – who made history. His great attraction as a cricketer was that he was an entertainer in an era when cricket managed to be both a serious profession and a game which was fun to play.

When Trueman walked out to bat, usually with Yorkshire needing quick runs to allow themselves to bowl out the opposition twice, he could be devastating with selective hitting and a defence which was sometimes so pronounced as to bring knowing smiles to those on the terraces who knew that for every forward defensive prod there would be havoc wreaked with a pull, a drive, or just a hook.

When Trueman was in the field he excelled at leg slip, fearless, agile, and not averse to reminding the batsman that he was there, lurking, awaiting the chance he knew would come his way.

Harold Wilson once named him the greatest living Yorkshireman and there were few who disagreed then or since. We will never again see his like.

Dickie Bird at the funeral of his great friend and cricketing colleague Fred Trueman.

Geoff Boycott – his friendship with Fred was restored.

Fiery Fred Trueman in typical action.

Subscribers

Stanley Abbey
David L Ackroyd
Howard Adamson
Jack Addison
Michael J Addison
Malcolm Douglas Addy
Richard Ainley
Mr F J Aitken
Norman Alderman
William Alderson
Christopher Thurman Allen
Richard Allison
Eric Allott
Laurence Alston
Robert D Ambler
Harold Amos
Gerry Ancell
Jeremy Anderson
John Aylmer Anderson
Mr Peter Andrew
David Andrews
Trevor K Andrews
Norman Armistead
David U Armitage
Stan Arnold
E M Arnold-Forster
Peter R Arrand
Paul L Arro
D S Ashbridge
Mr Richard Ashworth
John S Aspinall
Bill Asquith
Keith A Atkin
G D Atkinson
Robert Atkinson
Mavis Austin
Peter Austin
Esme E Avill
John M Avison
Peter Bagley
Roy Bailey
Kenneth Bailie
Geoff Bainton
Anthony G Baker
Graham Baker

Ralph Baker
Susan M Baker
Stuart Ball
Eric Balmforth
John Bamford
Donald Walker Bamforth
Peter Walker Bamforth
Albert Banton
Peter B Baren
Mr G T Bargh
Alan Barker (Rotherham)
Alan Barker (Halifax)
Colin C Barker
Dick Barker
Elaine M Barker
Stephen Barker
W Barker
Malcolm G Barker O.B.E
Peter Barnett
Tony Barrett
Jack Bates
Des Batty
Robert Baxter
Warner Baxter
D Beadle
Nigel Beadman
David Alexander Beal
David Michael Beal
Mrs Lyn Beale
Andrew B Beardsell
Gregory Beaumont
William Beck
John Beckett
Graham Beckwith
Godfrey Bedford
Mac Beevers
Sam Belcher
Christopher Anthony Bell
Michael Bell
Edward Bellringer
G Benfell
R Benfell
M J Bennet
Ben Bennett
Arthur John Benson

James Benson
Nathan James Benson
Roger H Benson
J W Bentley
Danny Bernstein
Noël Berry
Jack B Bethel
Arthur Bilsborough
John R Binks
Ruth Bird
Edward Birdsall
Terry Birtall
R J B Blake
Betty Blakeley
Ken Blakey
Mike Blanchard
Allan Blundell
Clive Bolsover
Nicholas Bolsover
Gordon Booth
Peter Booth
Raymond J Booth
Thomas P Booth
Barry Bootland
Richard Botting
Nesta Bottomley
Andrew J Bouldin
Allan Boulton
Stephen John Boulton
John Bowie
A M Bowmer
David M Bows
John W Bows
Alan Boyce
Ted Boyle
George William Boynton
Anthony Bradbury
Derek Bradby
Collin Bradford
E Bradley
Eric Bradley
Miss Jean Bradley
Joe Brandi
Miss K L Briggs
R Briggs

Paul Bright
Eric Britton
R F Britton
Noah John Broadbent
Scott Broadbent
The Reverend Thomas
Broadbent
David Broadley
Audrey Brooke
Malcolm N Brooke
Colin Brookes
Peter A Brookes
D Brooks
D Brown
Laurie Brown
Jamie D S Bryant
Robert Buckingham
Ian Buckley
L J Buckley
David Bullen
David A Burcombe
T R Burnham
Dr J M C Burton
J H Burton
Luke Burton
Michael Burton
Trevor Burton
Reginald Bush
Dr D R Butler
J H Butler
Malcolm Butler
E C Butt
Geoff Butterfield
John Buttery
Peter Byram
N P J Byrne
Paul Caddick
Paul Cambers
Frederick Canty
Derek Carpenter
Athel Carr
Jason Carr
Mrs Christine Carrington
David Cartwright
Mick Cartwright

Alan F Casson	Norman Crane	Peter Edmunds	Peter E Gant
Tony Caswell	V A Cranston	Kenneth W Elford	Joseph Ronald Garety
David P Cawthorn M.B.E.	John Crapper	Paul Elletson	D M Garside
Roger Cawthorne	Robert Crawford	Graham Elliott	Mr C E Gascoyne
Peter Chadwick	Robert C Crawley	Malcolm Elliott	David Gaunt (E Yorks)
Richard John Chaffer	B B Croft	Pamela M Elliott	David Gaunt (Birstall)
Rob Champion	David Lee Crole	Royce Elliott	Dr R M Gaunt
Graham Chaplin	L Crosland	Stuart Elliott	Roger & Pauline Gaunt
R W Chesman	Dr J C P Crowther	David Ellis	Dorothy Gibson
Ken Chilvers	Tony Cumiskey	Martin Ellis	Dr Tom Gibson
Neil Chilvers	Peter Cussons	R Ellis	Christopher Gilbert
A E Clamp	Frances Audrey Custance	James Wesley Ellison	Malcolm Gill
Antony Clark	Brian Dalby	Laurence Ellison	Steve Gill
G Clark	Denis G Dale	Paul Ellison	G N Gillingwater
Gordon Arthur Clark	G J Dalton	Peter A Ellway	John Gilroy
Olwyn & Francis Clarke	David Daniel	Basil Elsworth	Geoff Gittus
M Clayford	Eric Daniel	Michael Emery	Sophie Gittus
Alan Clayton	Mrs M Daniels	Martin Empsall	John Brian Gleave
Geoff Clayton	Stuart Davidson	Liam England	Mr M B Gleave
Mike Clegg	Barbara M Davies	Colin Evans	Phillip Gledhill
Peter Clegg	Gordon H Davies	John Evans	Mrs Peggy Glew
Alan Clough	Graham M Davies	Malcolm Evison	Ian M Goddard
Harry W Clough	Peter W Davies	Mrs S J Falls	Christopher Gooch
Ian Clough	Philip Davies MP	Robin Farrar	Michael Gooch
John A W Clough	Mike Davison	A J Faulkner	Terry Goodaire
Roy Clough	Keith Davy O.B.E	Gordon Fawcett	Betty L Goodchild
B J Coates	John F Dawson	Kenneth Fawcett	W M Goodwill
John Coates	S Dawson	John Fawcett	Christopher Goodwin
Roland Coates	Terence K Dawson	Frank Fawthrop	Adrian L Gough
Ronald Coates	Andy Day	Robert Fawthrop	P R Gouldsbrough
Roger Cogan	Eric Dean	Edward Featherstone	Ronald Goy
Terry Cogan	Eric Deighton	Ron Fell	Michael T Greaves
Patrick Colclough	John Dickens	Brian Fendley	Bernard Green
Stuart Coldwell	Ian Dodds	Brian Field	David Edward Green
Tom Collier	John Donnelly	Mike Field	R Green
Thomas R Collier-Taylor	Mrs Anne Doody	John Firth	William Green
F D Collins	Steve Doughty	Michael A Firth	Zoe Green
J Trevor Constantine	Dr M H Draisey	Mr Walter Firth	Ian Greenhalgh
Martyn Leslie Cooke	Clifford Drake	Simon Firth	N M Greenley
Richard Alan Cooke	Graham Dransfield	Elizabeth & Robin Fisher	Peter Greenwood
Stanley Cooke	Jack Driver	Paul Fisher	William Greenwood O.B.E
Terry Cooke	Richard Drury	Charles Foster	Ken Gregory
Bernard Cooper	M Duffield	John A Foster	Barbara E Griffiths
John Cooper	Maurice Duffield	Stephen G Foster	Ian Guilliat
Mrs C M Copeland	Graham Fielder Duffin	Brian Fowler	Chris Guthrie
Oliver Coulman	Dr Michael Dufton	Derek Fox	Brian Haddrell
Terry Cousins	Thomas Duncan	Ray Fox	Doug Haigh
John Andrew Coutts	Tony Dunlop	J T P Frankish	James Haigh
Norman Coverley	Michael Dykes	Michael Freeman	John Haigh
Andrew David Cox	Mr C J Dyson	Nancy Freeman	Brian Haley
David M Cox	Mr E C Dyson	Clifton Froggett	Christopher C Hall
Mrs C Coxah	David Earnshaw	Gerald A Full	Geoffrey Hall
Colin Crabtree	Joan Eastwood	Hon. Ald. D E Gabb O.B.E.	Nigel Hall
John H Cracknell	David Edgar	Peter J Gallivan	Patricia M Hall
Mike Craghill	Frank Edgeworth	Ted Gambles	Stan Hall

David Hall C.B.E TD
C H Halliday
Clement H Halliday
Douglas F Halliday
Joan Halliday
Martin Halsworth
John Hambleton
Ruth & William Hamby
George Phillip Hamer
Mary Hamer
Ken Hammill
Dorothy Ruth Hammond
Ken Hammond
John R Hampshire
Eric Hamshaw
Edward Handley
Colin Hanley
Kenneth E Hanson
Darren Hardaker
John Hardaker
Andrew Hardcastle
Jim Hardcastle
E Brian Hardgrave
Jack Hardwick
Duncon Hare
Florence Hargreaves
J W A Harker
Peter "Babe" Harris
Tim Harris
E Harrison
George H Harrison
Keith Harrison
Mo Harrison
Mr David J Harrison
Dick Hartley
Gordon A Hartley
Mark Andrew Hartley
Fred Haughey
Alan Hawke
J B Haworth
Eric Hawthorn
Alan Hayes
Malcolm L Hayton
Brian Hazelip
Peter Allan Heaney
John B Heath
Robert J Heath
Tony Hector
H Hedges
Stuart Hedley
Denis Heeley
Philip Hellawell
Michael F Helliwell
Tom Helme
Adam Hemingway

Chris Hemingway
Joe Henderson
Philip Hepworth
Anthony S Herrington
Bob Hesk
Harry Sherwin Hewitson
R A E Hickson
Bernard Hill
William Hill
John Hills
Ken Hillyard
J M Hirst
Philip A Hobkirk
J A Hodgskinson
Alan Hodson
Mr K R Hoggarth
Jonathan Holah
Gerald Holdroyd
Charles Douglas
Holdsworth
J Holdsworth
Jack Holdsworth
Chris Holland
Peter Holland
A D Hollindrake
Barry Hollingsworth
Frank Holmes
Jessie D Holt
Mike Holt (Rodley)
John Hooper
Paul S Hooper
Paul R Hope
Charles Hopkinson
Michael Horbury
Alan Hornby
Michael Horne
W Houlgate
David Howard
Graham & Julie Howard
John C Howard
Simon Howarth
Martin Howe
Paul Howley
Peter James Cleveland
Hoyle
H L Hudson
Tony Hudson
John Hughes
Philip Hughes
Michael Humphries
Graham Hunt
Peter B Hunt
Bryan H Hunter
Ian Ryder Hunter
Mr R B Hunter
C A Hurd

John V Hutchinson
R E L Hutchinson
Steve Hutchinson
John R Hutton
Nathan Idell-Lenton
Geoff Illingworth
Illingworth St Mary's C.C
Stuart Inman
Dr C M Irvin
Patrick Irwin
Eddie Isle
J Ison
Joan M Isted
Alan Jackson
Bernard Jackson
C L Jackson
B G Jacques
Kevin Jacques
Mrs Wendy Jameson
David Jaques
Michael Jeffery
David Jenkins
John Edward Jennings
Kevan B Jennings
Kevin Joel
Andrew A Johnson
Barry Johnson
Brian Johnson
E K Johnson
Graham Johnson
Ian Jones
Roy Jones
Jake Kay
David Kaye
Mrs Winifred Kaye
D M F Keith
Fred Kelly
Mr R E Kelly
Mr Sloan Kelly
Brian Kelsey
Paul Kelsey
D V J Kendall
Robert Kerrison
John Kershaw
Jeremy Kettlestring
A Philip Kilner
Mr Alan Kilner
Barry King
Isabel M King
Mr R King
A Kinghorn
James A A Kinghorn
Ian Kinnes
John R Kirby
Brenden Knowles

M S Knowles
Tony Lake
Mel Lamb
Robert A Lamb
John Law
Ian Lawrence
Peter H Lawrence
Keith Lawson
Mr W H P Laycock
E S Lea
Matthew Leach
Raymond Leach
Edric Leadbeater
Mr C M Leather
Major J M Lee T.D
David Leeming
Christopher M Lees
Mr Ron Lees
Jeffery Kitwood Leetham
Gordon Lethbridge
Geoff Lewis
Ian N E Lewis
Michael Lightfoot
Stuart Allan Lightfoot
Mr M M Lindley
J Lindley-Dawe
Tom R Lindsay
Hugh Lindsey
David Lister
Ron Lithgow
Rod Little
Ronald Lloyd
Morris Lockwood
Richard Lockwood
John S Lodge
Kathleen Logan
Roy Lomas
John Longbottom
James Lowe
David M Lowery
Gordon John Lunn
Jon Lunn
Mrs Hilda Lunn
K W Lynn
Agnes M Smith
David Main
Malcolm Main
Jenny Maisey
Roy Makinson
Stephen William Mallender
Terence John Mallender
J E Mallinson
Ged Maloney
Charles Manby
David Manby

John E Manby	Susan Moss	Kevan Portas	David Schofield
Paul Marlow	Matthew J Mould	David Poulter	N Schofield
Tim Marriner	John Mounsey	John Poulter	Richard Scott
David Marriott	J R Moverley	David Robert Powell	Alan Scruton
Malcolm S Marriott	David Mowforth	Brian Powley	Mr M Seel
J P Marsden	Richard Mumford	M Press	John M Sellers
Johnathan D Marsden	Paul Murgatroyd	John Pretlove	Colin Senior
Peter Marsden	Elle J Murray	David Priestley	Dr E Senior
Peter B Marshall	David B Myers	Peggy Priestley	David Sewards
Peter C Marshall	Howard N Myers	Anthony Prince	Mike Sewell
Sam and Harry Martin	Mel Neary	Robert Prudhoe	Alasdair Shaikh
Peter Mason	A G Nicholson	John Puddephatt	Mac Sharp
John Keith Maud	Stephen Nixon	Keith Purdy	Norman Sharp
Brian C Maw	Alec C Nunn	Rosie Pye	Mrs B Sharpe
John Maw	D Nussey	Robert K Radley	Peter Sharpe
R D Mawson	Aena E O'Reilly	John R Rains	Brian R Shaw
Keith McAvan	Gerald A O'Dowd	Gwen Rawling	Geoff Shaw
Gerard McDonough	Jeremy E Oates	Mrs Joan A V Rawling	Michael Shaw
David M McFarlane	William Oesterlein	Howard Ray	Dr Peter H W Sheard
Steven R McLean	Rob Oliver	Mr R Rea	John M Sheard
Roger McLeod	A Onion	Margaret Read	Marjorie Sheard
David McLoughlin	Mary & Peter Ormerod	Howard Rein	Denis Shearstone
Bernard McNulty	John H Osgerby	Owen Revis	Mr & Mrs D Sheasby
Nicola E McNulty	Richard J Packer	Fred Rhodes	Robert A Sheldon
Tony Medlicott	Lawrence Palfreeman	Kate Rhodes	Sheila A Shipstone
Terence Stephen Meegan	A G Parker	Rob Richardson	Michael J Shoesmith
Christopher John Mellor	Harry D Parker	Robin J Richardson	J H Shooter
Raymond Mellor	Betty Parkin	Simon Richmond	(decorator) Ltd
David John Memmott	John Michael Parkinson	Pierre Richterich	Greig Simms
John Mennell	M D Parkinson	Gerald L Ricketts	Michael Simms
Raymond Mennell	Derrick K Parrish	F A Riley-Smith	Neil Simms
George Merkin	Kevin Parry	Angus Rive	Jeffrey Simpson
Derek Metcalfe	Ajit Patel	George Malcolm Roast	Peter Simpson
George Metcalfe	Bernard P Payling	Alan J Roberts	Peter Michael Sizer
Malcolm Metcalfe	Fred Pearson	George Roberts	Keith Slater
Paul Metcalfe	John Pearson	William H Roberts	Wayne Slater
Val Metcalfe	Michael Pearson	John Robinson	James L Sleightholm
Keith Middleton	Richard Carlton Pearson	Phyllis T Robinson	Guy Smalley
Richard S Midgley	M I Penn	Shelagh J Robinson	Andrew Smallwood
Kenneth Mills	Jim Philipson	Gordon H Robson	Richard Smart
Robert Mirfield	Anthony W Phillips	Alan Roper	Agnes M Smith
Andy Mirfin	Don Phillips	Jonathan Gray Ropner	Barrie Smith
Robert A Mitchell	Bill Phillipson	Cyril Rothery	Charles Peter Smith
Gordon Moffatt	John Phipps	Mr W G Rounding	Clifford Smith
Jean Moody	Cyril M Pickup	Iain Rowe	Derek L Smith
Brian Moore	Margaret E Pigott	D Rowland	Don Smith
Dorothy Moore	Veronica Pikett	John Rowley	Dr Martyn Smith
Miss Dorothy Moore	Bryan Pilmer	Benjamin Rushton-Hooper	Geoffrey Smith
Vivienne Morley	M Pipes	Ian Ryder	Harold Smith
Robin E Morrell	Malcolm Pipes	Stephen Ryder	Howard Smith
William M Morrell	Kevin M Pitchford	John Sambrook	Howard G Smith
Mr David Morris	Ted Platt	Peter Samphire	Ivan Smith
Andrew Morrison	Don Player	John Samuel	Jeff Smith
Alan Morton	Norman Playforth	R J B Samuel	John and Brenda Smith
Roy Morton	Albert Poole	Colin Saunders	John H Smith

Kenneth G Smith
Malcolm Smith
Margaret Smith
Michael Smith
P A Smith
Peter Smith (Conisbrough)
Peter Smith
Peter H Smith
Philip Smith
Ray Smith
Raymond Smith
Robert Smith
Roy Smith
Terry & Jean Smith
Tony Smith (Laycock)
Barrie G Snoxell
Tim Soutar
C D Southwell
R V Southwell
Mr R Sparkes
Darren Speight
John D Spencely
John F Spencely
John M Spencer
Sam Spencer
Gavin Spiby
Norman Stabler
Derek Stacey
Allan Stalker
Geoffrey Stalker
R G Staniforth
Vernon Stansfield
Jeremy Stanyard
Miles Stanyard
Monica Stanyard
Michael Stark
Roger Statham
Dave Steel
Barry Stephenson
Robin Johnston Stewart
Roger Stewart
F R A Stirk
H Stockdale
Dennis Stockton
Chris Stone
Jim Stone
Michael Storey
Andrew Stott
J Stott
James A Stott
W B Stott
John Street
Norman Summersall
Godfrey Summers
Doreen & Theo Sumners

N R A Sutcliffe
Peter D Sutcliffe
Alan Sutherland
J Swales
Adam Swallow
Jean H Swift
Andrew Sykes
Mr J D (Bill) Sykes
Stuart Sykes
Christine Tadman
John Tate
Alec Taylor
Darren Taylor
J K Taylor
Ken Taylor
Mr E E Taylor & Mr E Taylor
Richard Taylor
Roger Taylor
Bill Thackray
Mrs Sally Theaker
Rodney Thewlis
Adrian Thompson
Geoff Thompson
George Thompson
Henry Thompson
Howard Thompson
John G Thompson
Leslie Thompson
Linda Thompson
Max Thompson
N Thompson
David Thorley
Dennis Thornhill
Brian & Mary Thornton
Colin Thorpe
Mr P F Tingle
Mick Tinker
John Todd
Mr & Mrs K R Tomlinson
Kevin Toolan
Stephen Tordoff
Joe Town
Ian Townsend
Tony Towse
Keiran Trotter
Michael Trotter
Herbert Walter Trousdale
Geoffrey Trueman
Sam & Molly Trueman
Albert Turner
Jack Turner
Mrs Marie Turner
Nick Turner
Malcolm Twigg
Jack Tyass

John Tye
R G Tyson
Eric D Umpleby
Barry E Upson
John R Utley
Anthony Valters
Robert Varley
Gordon Vickers
Pete Vickers
Andrew Vigrass
Chris Vigrass
Philip Vigrass
M G Vineall
Vollans Photography
Michael Waddington
Mr & Mrs J G Waddington
Mr W Waite
Revd. David Wakefield
Christopher Walker
David S Walker
James R Walker
Lawrence M Walker
Mr E Walker
Gary Waller
R G Walter
B S Ward
David M W Ward
F Ward
Frank Ward
Kit Ward
Martyn P Ward
Ian Ward (Thorner)
Jack Waring
Eleanor & Chris Warner
Matthew Wass
Sheila Waterworth
Barbara Watmuff
Bob Watson
Nellie & Ted Watson
K Weatherall
Brian Weatherhead
Margot Weaver
Gordon Webster
Richard A Webster
J M Wedgwood
Ron Weir
Clifford W Welburn
Robert H Welburn
Peter Wellington
John Wells
Richard Westcott
P Wetherald
Keith Whawell
Professor A D Wheatley
John Wheelwright

David W Whitaker
G D Whitaker
Paul Whitaker
J & K White
Richard White
Roy Whitehead
Robert Whiteley
Peter Whiteoak
Lesley D Widdop
Robin Wight
Mr E Wild
Andrew & Anne Wilkinson
Colin M R Wilkinson
G F "Yogi" Wilkinson
John Wilkinson
John G Wilkinson
Mike Wilkinson
Richard Wilkinson
H Willett
Mr William Edward Willey
Tony Williams
Peggy & Arthur Williamson
Edward J H Wilman
Gordon Field Wilson
John R Wilson
Mr Ken Wilson
Nicholas J Wilson
Nigel C Wilson
Geoffrey Wilson O.B.E.
Paul Winks
Harvey Winn
Alan S Wood
Andrew Keith Wood
David Wood
Don Wood
Howard Woodbridge
Nancy Wooler
Mrs J M Wormald
J B Worsnop
John A Worsnop
Alan Wrigglesworth
David S Wright
Gerry Wright
Stuart Wroe
Ian Yates
Ellis A Yeadon
Peter Yorke
Michael Ziff
Andrew
Mike
The Earl and Countess of Harewood